# The Well-Managed Sailboat

# THE WELL-MANAGED SAILBOAT

Equipping, Organizing and Maintaining Your Cruising Boat

George Day

HEARST MARINE BOOKS
*New York*

It is the policy of William Morrow and Company, Inc., and its imprints and affiliates, recognizing the importance of preserving what has been written, to print the books we publish on acid-free paper, and we exert our best efforts to that end.

Library of Congress Cataloging-in-Publication Data

Day, George, 1950-
    The well-managed sailboat: equipping, organizing and maintaining your cruising boat / George Day.
      p. cm.
    Includes index.
    ISBN 0–688–10665–X
    1. Sailboats—Equipment and supplies. 2. Sailboats—Maintenance and repair. I. Title.
VM351.D35   1992
623.8'223'028—dc20                                                          92–8301
                                                                              CIP

Printed in the United States of America

First Edition

1 2 3 4 5 6 7 8 9 10

BOOK DESIGN BY ARLENE SCHLEIFER GOLDBERG

# Contents

Preface     **9**

Introduction     **15**
▲ Protecting the Value of Your Boat     **17**
▲ Systems That Add Value     **18**
▲ Off-the-Shelf Versus Homemade Systems     **20**
▲ Dealing with Boatyards     **24**
▲ One Person's Experience Upgrading an Ocean-Cruising Yacht     **25**
▲ Conclusion     **31**

**Chapter One: Sail Handling Simplified**     **32**
▲ Setting Up Conventional Rigs     **34**
▲ Conventional Mainsail Options     **38**
▲ Conventional Mainsail Running Systems     **43**
▲ Conventional Headsail Systems     **49**
▲ Roller Furling-Reefing Headsails     **53**

▲ Roller Furling-Reefing Mainsails *59*

▲ Downwind Sails and Systems *61*

▲ Fully Automated Sailing Systems *65*

**Chapter Two: Deck Layouts That Work** *68*

▲ Sheets, Lines and Halyards *70*

▲ Anchors and Rodes *76*

▲ Big Items: Life Rafts, Windsurfers, Awnings, Etc. *78*

▲ Dinghies and Davits *85*

▲ Cockpit Struts and Arches for Radar, Solar Panels *89*
and Antennae

**Chapter Three: Anchoring the Easy Way** *94*

▲ Understanding Loads *96*

▲ The Right Anchors *99*

▲ Rodes for Cruising *105*

▲ Windlasses *110*

**Chapter Four: The Silent Crew** *114*

▲ Wind Vanes for Boats Under 50 Feet *116*

▲ Wind Vanes for Larger Boats *123*

▲ Autopilots *126*

**Chapter Five: The Command Center:
Navigation and Communications** *132*

▲ What Navigation Systems Should Do *134*

▲ Electronics for Coastal Cruising: Depth, Loran, RDF *137*
and Radar

▲ Electronics for Offshore Cruising: SatNav and GPS *142*

▲ Communications Afloat: VHF, SSB, Ham and EPIRB *145*

**Chapter Six: Engineering and Energy Systems** *152*

▲ Figuring Energy Needs and Battery Capacity *154*

▲ Engine-Driven Battery Charging *157*

▲ Simple On-Board Systems: Three Variations *158*

▲ On-Board Systems for Larger Boats *163*

▲ Living with the Diesel *169*

▲ Alternative Sources of Energy *171*

**Chapter Seven: Beating Barnacles and Blisters Below the Water** *178*

▲ Basic Precautions to Prevent Blisters *179*

▲ Renewing a Blistered Hull *183*

▲ Beating Barnacles with Antifouling Paints *185*

▲ Applying Bottom Paints *187*

▲ A Total Bottom System *189*

**Chapter Eight: The Comforts of a Floating Home** *191*

▲ The Galley *193*

▲ The Head *198*

▲ A Good Night's Sleep *201*

▲ The Main Saloon *206*

▲ Staying Warm and Dry *210*

▲ A Boat Is an Investment *212*

**Index** *215*

# PREFACE

It was a crisp October day when we left the dock at our home port of Newport, Rhode Island, to begin an extended cruise that would, over the next thirteen months, take us halfway around the world to New Zealand. Left behind on the dock were our best friends, our family, our jobs and our shoreside lives. Ahead was a new life aboard the high seas, brimming with the promise of adventure and discovery and underlined with uncertainty.

My wife, Rosie, and I were in our early forties. Our sons—Si, twelve, and Tim, nine—had been ensconced in a good school and had been leading busy lives playing sports on the local teams. I had been in the magazine business, most recently as editorial director for the magazines *Cruising World* and *Sailing World,* and Rosie had been a travel agent in a prosperous firm.

Life was good. But we had heard something that needed answering, something that called from far away and urged us to follow. I suppose it was in part the restlessness that overcomes some people in mid-life. But more than that, we all were called to do something together before it was too late. Our boys were growing up in spite of us, as our busy schedules and hectic strivings kept us all flying about in separate orbits. We saw each other at mealtimes, between the day's activities, and during evenings filled with homework and professional commitments. The clock seemed to be ticking faster and faster.

So we stepped off the edge of the earth. We sailed away for a while. It was a surprisingly easy decision, since sailing and cruising had been a part of our lives for a long while. We had owned a series of cruising boats and had spent many holidays cruising the coast of Maine or poking around the islands of the Caribbean on charter boats. The boys were just of an age when they were beginning to really understand how a boat works and how to manage the heavy gear and sails safely. Rosie and I were both fit and active. It was a natural way for us to do something exciting together.

I suppose I had more to do with the decision than the rest. I'd been voyaging and cruising offshore for twenty years and had once before taken part in a long sailing trip from the Caribbean to New Zealand. I had always harbored the notion that sailing with the family would make sense. Luckily they agreed. It happened on another crisp October day, when we were sailing a chartered 39-footer up Pamlico Sound in North Carolina. We had had a week of delightful sailing and had enjoyed each other's company so much that the idea to sail away sprang almost fully grown upon us and won without a fight.

But if it was easy to make the decision, what followed proved a challenge. We had to figure out how to finance the trip and we had to find a suitable boat. Even though I had been in the sailing business most of my working life and had spent more time than most sailors examining and sailing modern cruising boats, finding the right boat at the right price was difficult. We looked at dozens of craft from Maine to Florida and collected copious files crammed full with plans, magazine and newspaper clippings and brokers' fact sheets. In the end we did what I believe we should have done: We bought the boat we fell in love with. It was a Mason 43. I had written the boat review in *Cruising World* when the first 43 came in from Taiwan and had once spent two days at the Ta Shing yard in Tainan. I knew the boat and the builder and trusted both. We had to spend more than we wanted to, but we felt confident that with care and improvement the well-known brand would maintain its value when the time came to sell it. So the deed was done.

Financing an extended cruise depends upon where you are beginning. Most of those out cruising live off the profits of ongoing investments—real estate or businesses or stock portfolios. We weren't in that position and had to have a way to make ends meet while away.

To do that, we made a first simple decision: We sold all depreciating assets, such as cars and unneeded personal belongings, and kept all appreciating assets, such as our house, a few paintings and a vintage car. The giant yard sale in which we purged ourselves of twenty years of accumulation became a kind of Rubicon. With the house now only half full and a lump of cash sitting in a term deposit, we knew we couldn't turn back.

To supplement the cruising kitty, I set up writing work that would keep me busy at the laptop computer and bring in a steady flow of cash. *Cruising World* allowed me to write the monthly column "On Watch," tracing the course of our voyage as we wended our way about the world. Without the support of *Cruising World*'s publisher, John Southam, and editor, Bernadette Bernon, we wouldn't have got as far as we have. Also, I was lucky enough to strike up a similar arrangement with *Islands* magazine's editor, Joan Tapper, who took a fancy to our voyage and has been running my "High Seas Letter" in most issues.

Writing for a living is a dicey business and one that can be hard to crack and even harder to make much of a profit from. For those who look to their typewriters as a source of income, all I can advise is to get to know your markets as well as you can, make yourself useful to editors who are looking for material you can provide, and then produce reliably publishable work. Learning a trade such as diesel mechanics, haircutting, refrigeration repair, electronics repair or sail-making will be much more rewarding.

On the October morning we left, we had our hearts in our throats. It was a dead-calm Sunday with clear skies and a hint of frost in the air. We motor-sailed southward toward Long Island Sound, covering familiar waters, sailing by well-known harbors, but seeing it all with fresh eyes. This was the beginning, and our senses were as sharp as razors.

We spent two months on the East Coast and then sailed southward for Jamaica and Panama. In March we sailed out into the Pacific and cruised westward with the trade winds for seven months until we reached Fiji. There we turned south to New Zealand, where we could escape the South Pacific's hurricane season and spend time with our many extended-family members and friends.

The trip up to that point was not remarkable in any way, except in what it meant to us. Cruising and voyaging had brought us together as a family in a new way. We had done things we were afraid we might not be able to do. We'd rediscovered the simple pleasures of reading aloud and taking long walks. Children and parents learned to rely on each other as members of a team, to talk frankly about what needed doing and to listen carefully to what was being said. As we became more self-sufficient, our confidence grew. The world seemed a brighter and better place.

It was through the months of preparation and the year of cruising that the bones of this book came together. I've now owned a series of boats and have cruised some 40,000 miles. We've learned a thing or two, but we still have much to discover and much to learn. My hope is that in these pages there will be morsels here and there that will help sailors like us who want to spend time cruising, whether along the coast over the weekend or out on the high seas. If life aboard a cruising boat can be made more comfortable, if sails can be trimmed more effectively, if the systems that keep it all going can be laid out logically and practically, then cruising can be a wonderful life. It has been for us. And we're eagerly getting ready to get under way again when the hurricane season ends. We still have farther to sail.

George Day
Waimate, South Canterbury
New Zealand

# The Well-Managed Sailboat

# INTRODUCTION

*Use a systems approach to fit out and upgrade your cruising sailboat.*

▲ Protecting the Value of Your Boat

▲ Systems That Add Value

▲ Off-the-Shelf Versus Homemade Systems

▲ Dealing with Boatyards

▲ One Person's Experience Upgrading an Ocean-Cruising Yacht

Sailing free across an open body of water is a pastime filled with magic. The wind creases the water, the tall mast stands high and the smartly curved sails catch the wind, harness it and transform it into power that urges the hull below through the water. No machine drones as you sail—only the wind blowing in your hair and at the taut edges of the sails that spirit you on.

In itself sailing might seem the simplest and possibly the purest form of travel. Surely it is the most natural and traditional. Yet sailing and owning and setting up a sailboat is a complicated endeavor. It can take a lifetime to explore the limits of sailing and cruising. This is true because a sailboat is that strange anomaly: It is the simplest of creatures, yet it has contained in it many complex and often cranky devices, setups and configurations of gear, lines and equipment.

A cruising sailboat may be the most elegant expression of our ability to harness nature to utilitarian purposes. Sailors have been working to perfect the art for thousands of years. Solid and sometimes rigid traditions have come down to the recreational sailors of today, most of which are based on good and valuable experience. But in many cases it no longer makes sense to do things the way the old salts did them. Times have changed. Boats and gear have changed. And our ability to solve problems aboard with gear, technology and new techniques has evolved rapidly. In the last two decades we have seen a virtual revolution in the development of gear and equipment for sailboats. Nothing to do with sailboats has remained unchanged. And in almost every area of this revolution in sailing we have seen new gear and techniques developed that make the average sailor's time on the water better and happier. We sail faster than ever. We stay drier and warmer. We find our way across the sea more accurately. And the crew has never been safer at sea.

The purpose of this book is to open doors for the reader, to help those who have just got into their first cruising boat solve the basic problems of fitting out the boat and to help more experienced sailors take their boats to a level of preparation suitable for extended sailing offshore. In many instances the solutions to problems will involve the application of new gear. Yet we will also look into techniques that will give novices in particular a few tricks of the trade to make sailing easier and simpler.

Because cruising sailboats, which today tend to be fitted out with many different types of equipment, are complicated, a newcomer can easily become overwhelmed with details and lose the big picture of what he or she is trying to accomplish. Even those of us who have owned boats and cruised the world for years can find ourselves mired in detail and confronted by problems we cannot solve. To keep the whole boat in perspective and to maintain an orderly approach to upgrading and fitting out a boat, it is wise to use what we'll call the systems approach to organizing and working on your boat.

A systems approach is nothing especially exotic. The term is technobabble for doing what nature does automatically—group flora and fauna and the inert world of elements together into logical and consistent groups. We'll do the same with the elements of a cruising sailboat, linking areas aboard that make sense together. As a run-through of the table of contents of this book shows, we have covered just about every aspect of fitting out a new or used boat for coastal and offshore cruising. We have made every effort to select the systems that will make the most difference to you and those who sail with you and those that will add as much value as possible to your boat.

## PROTECTING THE VALUE OF YOUR BOAT

For many of us, our boats represent the second-largest purchase in our lives, following our homes. Value is very important. While you may have just purchased a boat or may be looking for a new boat, the fact of the matter is that within five to seven years your new boat will more than likely be back on the market again. On average, boats are sold and resold every four and a half years. There was a time, twenty years ago, when a boat owner could reasonably expect to sell his or her boat for as much or more than he paid for it. As values in boats increased, in those years, we saw more and more owners moving up to larger boats. But unfortunately today many boats on the market do not maintain their value and in fact depreciate in much the same way an automobile depreciates. It is common for inexperienced owners to lose as much as 40 percent of the initial value of a brand-new production cruising boat during the five years they own it.

This does not need to be the case. It is possible to buy a boat—new or used—to fit it out to meet your sailing needs and requirements, to sail as far as you please and back again and then sell it at a fair value without losing your shirt. The difference between losing 40 percent on a boat and breaking even or making money lies entirely with the owner.

First, if you have bought a boat for which there is a reasonably active market and a local market in your region of the country, you're off to a good start. You may have your heart set on a wonderful cruiser designed by a little-known foreign genius and built by an unknown builder in a faraway land. The boat may suit your needs admirably. But if it is the only one in your sailing region, if no one has ever heard of the boat's brand, never heard of the builder and never heard of the designer, you will have a hard time selling the boat again when that time comes. By purchasing a unique and unknown boat, you almost ensure a loss in value. This of course is not the case with "gold-platers"—large charter vessels and exotic and highly expensive custom cruising designs. These boats make their own market and hold their value if they are well maintained no matter where they are sailed and how unique they may be.

The converse is true of racing boats. Sailboats that have been designed to a rule tend to lose value as they lose their competitive edge. A tired five-year-old racing machine, which is laden with hardware and dozens of sails, may not be worth the value of the gear on board. The rig and spars may be on the verge of needing replacing. The hull and the hull-keel joint may have lost a lot of their original integrity. The deck may be flexing, and the gear bolted to it may be tired. A 45-footer that cost $300,000 to build and fit out might not fetch $100,000, if it can be sold at all. In these cases all the value in the boat has been spent around the buoys and little is left for second and third owners.

If you have taken the trouble to improve the boat with gear and equipment—cruising systems—that have lasting value in the used boat market, if you have taken the trouble to maintain the boat well and keep abreast of repairs, and if you have purchased a boat with a known market, then you should be able to protect your value in the boat. One of our purposes here will be to aid you toward that end.

## SYSTEMS THAT ADD VALUE

In the residential real estate market you will hear savvy investors repeat three buzzwords of advice for those who want to succeed in the business: location, kitchens and bathrooms. Those are the elements that have the biggest impact on a property's value in the market. While you are improving your boat to make it a better cruising boat for coastal and offshore sailing, it is wise to keep in mind that there are some systems you can add that will hold or increase the boat's value and some that will lose their value quickly.

The value of a boat is more than simply what it will draw on the market when put up for sale. The selling price is one excellent measure of a boat's value. But it is only one aspect. In the discussion that follows and throughout this book, when we talk of value, we'll be talking about how well boats, gear, equipment and installations fit the basic requirements of the sea: in other words, how appropriate and seamanlike they are; how safe, strong, functional and attractive. The old term *Bristol fashion* describes the value intended here. A boat that has been equipped and is kept in Bristol fashion is a better and more trouble-free cruising boat and draws more on the market than does her less well equipped and cared for sister: that's value.

The additions you buy for your boat that will hold their value include: simplified sail-handling systems, such as roller furling; easy anchoring systems, such as a robust windlass and appropriate anchors; modern galley systems, such as a propane stove with an oven and a refrigerator; and up-to-date electronics in the cockpit and navigator's station.

Items that you may want to add to your new boat that probably will not help you maintain the boat's value include: hull graphics; specialty sails, such as downwind twins and their poles; interior decor, such as pictures on the bulkheads, cushions, pillows and rugs; inexpensive galley gear, such as pots and pans, plates and cutlery; and lastly any system that requires special knowledge on the part of the operator, such as a ham radio or an exotic, nonstandard battery-charging system.

What is the difference between systems that keep their value and those that don't? The answer lies first in how well the gear serves you when put to the trial at sea. It must be made of durable and corrosion-resistant materials. It must be well engineered for use at sea and incorporate features that make it safe and convenient. If the gear or equipment is in relatively common use, is well made and is designed for use at sea, it should improve your experience on the water and add value to your boat.

There is a second important measure of value as well. How will a potential buyer five years down the track measure the worth of your boat? What will he be looking for? Probably he or she will be interested in many of the same things that concerned you when you went boat hunting. In most cases the person will be looking for a boat to sail with a spouse, family and friends, and his first concerns will be for their safety, comfort and well-being. In surveys of new boat buyers more than half of all boats sold were finally selected by a wife who was choosing from a short "A-List" provided by her husband. In other words the boat has to serve the needs of the whole crew, which is often the whole family.

Once satisfied that the boat is seaworthy and comfortable, that future buyer of your boat will want to be assured that it will perform up to his expectations. Is it as fast and sea-kindly as reputed and equipped to make the best of its potential? The sail inventory and sailing systems will be key here. But just as important in the notion of performance is the engine, propeller and steering systems. If the boat is a dog under power or is difficult to steer because of a poorly designed steering system, it will be more difficult to sell.

And lastly the potential buyer will be interested in the quality of the gear, hardware and systems on board, and how these are installed and maintained. Money-saving but little known gear will not hold its value, whereas gear with a solid reputation will. Gear that has been improperly installed, or installed in an unorthodox way, will also be diminished in value. Systems that have been cobbled together from hardware-store supplies are worse than worthless to a new owner, for he will more than likely have to remove the homemade whatsit before replacing it.

Protecting the inherent value in your boat requires investing in the right systems and in the right gear. That's not to say that fitting out a boat needs to be a job fraught with agonizing investment decisions. It should be fun, first, or it's not worth doing. Secondly it should be seamanlike, or we'd be forgetting the traditions of sailing and the sea. Only lastly should the boat's resale be of real concern.

Yet, for most of us, we will be happier out sailing, happier working on the boat and happier paying the bills from the boatyard and chandlery if we're reasonably assured we're not going to lose our shirts when we finally decide to sell the boat and move on to the next one.

## OFF-THE-SHELF VERSUS HOMEMADE SYSTEMS

The approach we take to fitting out a boat for coastal and offshore cruising will have a real bearing on how well the gear and boat behaves out on the open water and, again, on the value of the boat at the end of the day. If you are an inveterate do-it-yourselfer, you will be tempted to tackle many fitting-out tasks yourself and will use materials at hand and ingenuity to solve problems. But if you are like most of us, you will only have a certain amount of skill and less time to tackle projects, so off-the-shelf systems or boatyard-built systems will be your route to problem solving.

Do-it-yourselfers often come up with ingenious solutions to problems. You will see PVC pipe used to hold all types of things on deck, from fishing poles to man-overboard dan buoys to Danforth-style anchors. You will see common garden hoses split in half and used as chafe gear in the rigging and nailed to the gunnels of dinghies. And you'll see milk crates from dairies around the country stuffed with anchor lines and other gear and tied on deck or used as organizers in deck lockers.

The variety of such homemade fixes is as unlimited as the imagination. In most cases when nonmarine items are used to solve problems afloat, the installation will be a bit rough around the edges. While a piece of PVC might work fine as an anchor chalk, it will never look as good or work as well as a stainless-steel bow chalk tailor-made for the anchor. The most obvious difference, in this instance, is price—$20 worth of pipe and hose clamps versus $125 worth of stainless-steel parts.

But there is also a difference in value. A PVC tube will provide a quick fix to the problem of where to stow your Danforth-style anchor on the pulpit of a small cruising boat. But it will not add value to your vessel and will in fact detract from the actual value of the boat. The reason is that such homemade deck gear—unless expertly made and fitted—will not be a solution for the next owner, who may well not want to have PVC pipe hose clamped about the boat. The difference in value, then, is in the quality of the materials and the appropriateness of the application. While PVC might work, a cantilevered stainless-steel bow roller fitted to the anchor is better and will add to the overall value of your boat.

The same difference in value applies to the installation of furniture, gear and electronics belowdecks. Most of us are tempted to save money by building in our own bookshelves, wineglass racks and so forth. Some of us even install our own electronics, wiring, plumbing and other systems. If you have the needed knowledge to install gear and equipment well, then doing jobs yourself can save a lot of money. But if you don't have the skill and have not done much shipwright work or yacht joinery, you may well find that you have made a muddle of an installation, and despite the inherent value of the gear you've installed, you've detracted from the boat's value.

With these comments I do not intend to disparage do-it-yourselfers who are real craftsmen. No doubt many readers will be capable of tackling complex projects on their own—from carpentry to metalwork to engine-room mechanical work. If the work they do is of Bristol quality, then they will be adding value to their boats. Moreover if you are handy and plan to sail to areas where you need to be self-sufficient, it is prudent to learn how your systems work from the inside out before you go—by installing them.

For the majority of boat owners, however, it may well be wise to think hard before tackling a fitting-out or upgrading project in an area for which you have little or no expertise. The best approach when confronted with such a project is to look at off-the-shelf solutions provided by gear and equipment manufacturers who are involved in sailing and boat ownership. In other words, if you decide to rewire your electrical panel, it would be more prudent to purchase a premade panel from a reputable company than to opt for the possibly cheaper solution of building a board from circuit breakers and plywood.

Or, in another instance, if you decide to add lazy jacks, you may well do better to purchase one of Harken's Lazy Jack systems and install it than to puzzle through all the fittings and splices yourself. The difference in the performance between homemade lazy jacks and store-bought varieties may not be very great. But the durability, precision and look of well-engineered blocks, splices and lines will do the job better than lazy jacks cobbled together from line and materials on hand.

Anyone who has visited one of the major boat shows can attest to the wide and ingenious variety of marine gear available to solve just about every on-board problem—from bilge pumps, to solar water heaters, to sophisticated devices for charging batteries, to a wide array of systems for controlling mainsails and jibs. If you want to organize your boat in a certain way, if you have conceived of a system that will make life on board better, have a look around at the marketplace and in almost every instance you will be able to find gear dedicated to the installation you have in mind. The explosion in new gear in the last decade has been enormous. Established companies have come out with hundreds of new products, as they have been challenged on every side by innovators who want to stake out a place in the sailing business. While the end of the 1980s and early 1990s saw some businesses fail during the lean, recessionary years, sailors today still have much more to choose from than ever before.

Quality off-the-shelf gear is not all the same, nor is price. While it is generally true that you get what you pay for, you will find that prices vary widely for even simple deck hardware. Catalog houses have been able to drop retail prices to near-wholesale levels, forcing neighborhood chandleries to trim their prices as well. And manufacturers who are having their gear built and assembled offshore have been able to introduce gear and equipment at prices that are hard for U.S. companies to match. In all this variety of outlets and items, it can be difficult to find just what will serve your needs best.

The best approach when buying off-the-shelf gear is to research the available gear and various prices carefully. You will have to set your own price point, but it should be obvious that you need to buy quality as well as price if you want the purchase to add value to your sailing and to your boat. You don't always have to buy top-end products, nor should you buy all bargain-basement products. Look for name-brand products with solid reputations; learn about the gear from brochures, catalogs and magazines; and then buy the best value.

Buying all top-of-the line gear will give you many performance edges and should help to preserve the long-term value of the boat. Yet be certain that you are getting what you pay for, that innovations aren't crippled by bugs in the design and that the company's marketing department hasn't jumped months ahead of the manufacturing department in promoting a product that isn't really reliable enough to be on the market. It happens. And no one wants to go to sea depending on a prototype.

On the flip side, if you are seeking the lowest price and lowest performance in a piece of gear, you may also discover that you end up with the lowest level of reliability. To make an item durable in a harsh marine environment requires the use of appropriate materials, engineering and craftsmanship. These cost the manufacturer money, which in turn costs the retail customer money. If you find a no-name product that is priced well below the name brands, take a good hard look at the product's quality before spending money on it—find out where the gear was manufactured, by whom and under what level of supervision.

And if you see a piece of no-name equipment or gear in a mail-order catalog—even the most reputable catalog—which seems to suit your needs at a very reasonable price, don't rush to the phone. You're bound to be disappointed. Unless you have had a hard look at the gear or have had favorable recommendations from a source you trust—friends, magazines and so on—you have no way of judging the item's quality.

Off-the-shelf gear and equipment today has been refined to the point that you should be able to find something to fit just about any need. You should be able to find products from reputable companies at reasonable prices. In today's market it is possible at every turn to add value to your boat while making it easier and more fun to sail.

## DEALING WITH BOATYARDS

There are many instances on board when you will find that your new systems do not quite fit into or onto your boat. And you may have a concept that the off-the-shelf market can't totally solve. In that situation you'll more than likely turn to your boatyard or local boatwrights, joiners, mechanics and other experts to work out solutions.

Building in custom gear and custom installations will be both fun and expensive because, more often than not, you will be installing off-the-shelf items in unique and difficult ways, requiring a lot of yard time—at $30 to $50 an hour. The most important thing to think about when you decide to have custom work done is choosing the right craftsmen and right yard for the jobs. Although you may already be using a yard to haul your boat and may be friendly with the guys who work there, you may well do better to look at the yard up the river or across town to get special work done, simply because your home yard does not have the craftsmen you require. Look around, shop around. Get quotes from several yards and bargain. You will find that having work done during slow seasons—from November to March in the northern climates, for example—will be less expensive and of better quality than work done during the launching season.

When dealing with most boatyards, planning and patience are important qualities to master. Boatyards are service companies that almost all run on the squeaky-wheel principle. The clients who raise the biggest ruckus (and often have the biggest boats) get the quickest attention. If you show up during the busy season with several small (low profit for the yard) jobs and stand back meekly waiting for your work to be done, you'll find the sailing season slipping by before your eyes.

That's not to advise anyone to be a squeaky wheel. A better approach in our experience is to determine the yard's slow periods and plan to have large jobs done then. If that means losing a week of sailing at the end of the season so that the yard can get an early start, so be it. Better that than losing a month at the other end.

The second basic piece of advice when dealing with boatyards is to write down everything you want done and make sure both you and the yard manager have copies. It is wise to include in such "memos" or "letters" as much detail as possible. You should specify the brands of gear you want if possible and detail the installation as carefully as you can. A clear sketch supplied by the owner with a list of materials will help the manager and yard staff do the job you want. Moreover when the job is finished, both you and the yard have a benchmark against which to measure the final outcome. Having a plan in writing will enable the yard manager, who will probably know a lot about the equipment and installation you have in mind, to contribute his thoughts and experience to the project. As the plan evolves, be sure to keep updated notes on what you actually intend to do. Otherwise you will find yourself uncertain about how the project should end up and uncertain about the price.

Patience is always useful when dealing with a boatyard. Like family farms, boatyards are often shorthanded when the heaviest work needs to be done. And they are always at the mercy of the weather. If you are having some painting done out in the open and it rains for a week, you and a dozen other owners will fall behind schedule. It just happens that way. Being a squeaky wheel won't stop the rain or add any more hours to the day.

The work done by most reputable yards will be in "yacht style," or Bristol fashion. Unless you are having very unusual custom work done—say, a deck crate for your motorcycle—you will find that boatyard installations of gear will add to your boat's performance and value. When compared with an amateur, do-it-yourself job, the professional work will always carry the day. Professional work may be expensive, but quality work in substantial upgrades of on-board systems will help you maintain the value of your boat.

# ONE PERSON'S EXPERIENCE UPGRADING AN OCEAN-CRUISING YACHT

To offer an idea of the thought processes and decisions that can be involved when outfitting a boat and upgrading cruising systems, I will sketch out the work we did aboard *Clover*, our Mason 43, in the eighteen months prior to setting off for an extended cruise around the world. Although the cruise we embarked upon is not a typical one for most sailors—from Newport, Rhode Island, to New Zealand via

Panama and return—the basics we had to cover outfitting the boat will be familiar to just about everyone who coastal-cruises or ventures offshore.

We were starting with an advantage because the boat had been quite well fitted out by its first owner and had then been thoughtfully upgraded by its second owner. Built in 1980 and launched in Europe in 1981, the boat had been sailed across the Atlantic Ocean six times and back and forth from the Caribbean to the East Coast of the United States twice. She was well fitted out, well tested at sea, and just a bit tired. Because of that and because the seller was eager to move on to new projects, we were able to purchase the boat at about the bottom of the Mason 43–class price range.

That's just what we wanted. We intended to upgrade the boat significantly and bring her finish up to a high polish. We intended to restore her, over time, to her original Bristol fashion. It was not a small undertaking, one we were not skilled enough nor had time enough to tackle entirely on our own. We would do most of the projects, but many we would farm out to specialists and our boatyard. Just keeping track of it all was a job in itself. In the process the systems approach was born.

Here's how we approached each system.

1. *Sails and Rigging:* The boat was to be sailed by a family of four, two adults and two children. Our boys, twelve and nine, were helpful but could not at the start be counted as full crew members. Thus we needed a rig that effectively could be handled by a singlehander— either Rosa or me alone on watch—and for which the watch stander rarely had to leave the cockpit. The basic addition, then, was a roller-reefing/roller-furling headsail system. We went with the ProFurl 42, which had worked well on BOC Round The World boats and had our genoa and Yankee fitted with a luff tape and with luff padding, which would take up some of the sails' bagginess as they were reefed.

We already had a self-tacking staysail, installed by a previous owner, which is a delightful sail when maneuvering in tight quarters or going to weather in winds over 30 knots. We made no changes to this. Also with the boat we inherited twin downwind running sails, virtually unused by both previous owners, and the two poles that went with them. I have used twins and object to the long setup time they require and to the vicious rolling they cause in a boat with a deep keel such as *Clover's.* So we cut one of the sails into a new Yankee and stored the other for future use. In their place we purchased a used spinnaker

(950 square feet/$600), lengthened one of the poles to our full J-measurement and purchased a spinnaker sock. We use the spinnaker in winds up to 10 knots apparent (17 knots true), and it drives *Clover* at hull speed in anything over 12 knots true wind speed. We love the sail and keep all lines for it rigged all the time.

Moving aft, we decided to use full battens in the main and mizzen, to ease wear and tear and to improve sail shape. This system, coupled with lazy jacks, makes dousing and furling both sails a snap, even in strong breezes. Even though I like the simplicity of our system, I have often gazed fondly at roller-furling mains, while remembering all those times I wanted to take in only a foot or so of sail and not tie in a whole second or third reef.

In the rig itself we had the rigger at our boatyard inspect all swage fittings, turnbuckles, terminals and the masts and booms carefully. He reported that the mizzen spreaders had hairline cracks; that the main cap shrouds, forestay and backstay showed corrosion in the swagings, and that the intermediates and lowers were fine. Following his advice, we had the yard replace the cap shrouds, forestay and backstay with MacWhyte stainless-steel wire (⅜ inch) and Navtec terminals, all supplied by Hall Spars. These were jobs I wanted completed by professionals.

*2. Deck Layout:* When you buy a used boat, you normally have systems on deck put there by previous owners. In our case we had the self-tending staysail arrangement, plus an arrangement for staysail sheets and halyards to lead aft. Otherwise the layout was fairly orthodox, with halyards at the mainmast, sheets aft, and guys, downhauls and so forth as temporary arrangements. We needed to do several things: arrange for a lot of deck stowage, since the cockpit lockers are small; arrange protection from the weather in the otherwise open cockpit; and add a second working anchor on the bow.

For deck storage we had a shipwright friend of ours construct two low-profile deck boxes, screwed to the deck on the cabin top on either side of the mainmast. These are catchalls for deck gear—everything from chain hooks to Avon dinghy pumps, shell collections to sail stops and deck tools. They are reorganized periodically but are basically filled with whatever fits into them. For larger items—the sail board, two masts, two sails, boogie boards, fishing rods and other bulky items—we had a canvas bag sewn up that stands against the foredeck lifelines. We call it the garage, and like a garage it tends to house more than it was designed for.

For protection we added only a pramhood over the companionway—the boat is not suited to a normal dodger—and enclosed the cockpit with weather cloths and a sun awning under (or over) the mizzen boom.

Lastly the boat still had its original winches. Since Rosa was destined to be a lone watch stander, we needed to have powerful self-tailing winches. We accomplished this with the help of the boat's builder, Pacific Asian Enterprises, who recommended Lewmar 46s and supplied them to order. We now can handle the genoa and spinnaker single-handed and are able to reef the headsail to a tiny scrap in a blow without trouble.

3. *Anchors and Tackle:* We already had a 75-pound plow on ⅝-inch chain. We replaced the ⁵⁄₁₆ with ⅜-inch BBB, tied to the plow with a heavy swivel. For our second working anchor we used a 44-pound Bruce, with 20 feet of ⅜ BBB chain and 200 feet of ⅞-inch nylon line. Both anchors sit on the double roller that came with the boat and can be worked either together or independently on the huge Lofrans Atlas windlass on the bow (my favorite piece of gear on the boat). In addition we use a 12-pound Danforth-style anchor, kept in a cockpit locker as our stern anchor.

For our storm anchor (in addition to the 75-pound plow we use on our working tackle) we have a 75-pound Danforth-style anchor, 250 feet of nylon rode, and 100 feet of chain stowed below the floorboards. Our strategy, in the likelihood of a dangerous storm, will be to seek a safe anchorage and then set three anchors in the anticipated direction of the storm's wind shifts. Friends call this overkill. We just call it a good night's sleep.

4. *Self-steering:* We had plans to sail quite a few miles with only ourselves for crew, so we needed a reliable form of self-steering to relieve ourselves of the most onerous task for ocean voyagers: steering. *Clover* was equipped with a Sailomat wind-vane unit when we bought her—one of the reasons we settled on the boat. This unit had steered the boat some 35,000 miles and has continued to steer her a farther 11,000 miles without a breakdown. We've subsequently added a small Autohelm 3000 autopilot for use while powering or in light downwind conditions. The Autohelm draws so few amps we barely notice its effects on our house batteries.

5. *Navigation and Communications:* With *Clover* came two generations of electronics and communications. The first owner, a European who cruised to the Caribbean, had put aboard a good depth sounder,

log and speedo, a VHF radio, an excellent ADF (automatic direction finder), particularly useful in Europe, where radio direction finding is a staple of coastal cruising, an early Combi SatNav and a high-seas shortwave receiver. To this the second owner added a top-quality Loran. We were satisfied with the setup, and found the gear, although used and in some cases low-tech, to be reliable and efficient.

However, we were straying farther afield and we were setting off in the age of GPS. So on top of the existing equipment we added a Magellan GPS unit, upgraded to the 1000 level, and a full-frequency SSB/ham radio (an ICOM 720A, which is no longer manufactured but is an excellent radio).

We rarely pull out our sextant anymore, except to keep our skills up. We keep our position at sea with a minimum of two corresponding fixes, mostly SatNav and GPS, and keep a running DR as well. We are able to talk virtually all over the world via radio and can receive worldwide time signals and weather reports on either the shortwave receiver or the SSB. We've built in some redundancy, which we believe lends a measure of safety.

6. *Engineering Systems:* There are several different approaches to take when designing the basic engineering systems of a cruising boat, which are based on how the boat is to be used. Boats that will be in marinas and attached to electricity require one setup; boats that are moving regularly and are seldom in marinas—such as bareboat charter boats—require a second type of setup; and larger boats with room for ample systems require a third approach.

Aboard *Clover* we had a simple system to start with—no refrigerator, no water maker, no generator—with only a 30-amp alternator charging 300 amp/hours of batteries running off the main 65-hp engine. Hot fresh water is heated in the 6-gallon tank via plumbing running off the freshwater side of the main engine's cooling system. We do have pressure water and a wide array of houselights, some of which use 20 watts. We knew we would be traveling and that we wanted as simple a setup as possible. Also we knew we wanted a refrigerator-freezer.

So the simplest approach for us was to increase our battery reservoir to 450 amp hours with a new 4D gelcell on the house side of the bank. This, then, would be charged with a new high-capacity alternator (110 amps maximum with about 60 amps actual at regular revs). We did not go for a regulator bypass for quick charges, since we would be running the engine anyway to operate the refrigerator. We can also use a small 500-watt Honda gas generator to top up the batteries if need be.

The refrigerator-freezer system is solely engine-driven. We installed a Sea Frost spillover system that basically divided our existing ice chest into two halves, with one being the freezer and the other being the refrigerator. It requires about two hours a day of engine running in the tropics to keep the freezer down. In higher latitudes that drops to about an hour per day.

Running the engine for an hour provides us with approximately 60 amps, which is our average daily draw. Two hours gives us about 90 amps, as the regulator decreases output as voltage in the battery banks increases toward maximum.

For living aboard and active use, this system—modeled on bareboat charter boats—works fine. More battery capacity would be useful, for, as they say, you can't have too many amps. The other more complex and high-tech systems will be discussed in more detail in the chapter on engineering systems.

7. *Underwater—Blisters and Paint:* Like many boat owners, we were concerned that we not lose our investment or find ourselves with a major repair job due to blisters under the water. Also, we knew we would be leaving the boat in the water for eighteen months before hauling for a repaint job, so we needed to coat the bottom with a system to prevent barnacles and ward off blisters.

We did this by grinding off all the old bottom paint and covering the bottom with a thick epoxy barrier coat. Over this we rolled on three coats of Pettit's Trinidad bottom paint, which has the highest concentration of copper on the market. The paint worked well for fourteen months in the tropics. The epoxy undercoat should protect the bottom for years.

8. *Comforts of Home:* We planned to live aboard *Clover,* so we spent time and money making her accommodations as homey as we could. We had new cushions made all around the boat and covered them with a durable, stain-resistant fabric. For each of the six berths we planned to use (the boat can sleep nine!) we made two sets of form-fitted sheets with Synchilla blankets. We installed reading and mood lights and hooked up outlets for 12-volt appliances. We hung pictures on the bulkheads and tossed area rugs over the teak and holly cabin sole. The net effect was to transform a comfortable but impersonal interior into a place a family could call home, a transformation that

meant a great deal to the success of the voyage ahead and can make a great difference to the way any family or crew feels about time cruising.

All of this took about eighteen months and many hundreds of hours of work by us, by craftsmen we hired and by our boatyard. The final cost of fitting out and upgrading *Clover*, including a new dinghy and outboard, came to approximately 25 percent of the purchase price of the boat. We had added value to the basic Mason 43, had improved it and made it ready for ocean voyaging. That percentage is typical of new boat owners who are preparing their vessels for coastal and offshore sailing.

## CONCLUSION

By using a systems approach, by buying carefully and then upgrading the boat in a way that adds value to the vessel, you will be able to enjoy your time on the water better than if you go about the business of boat ownership haphazardly. In the chapters that follow we will discuss basic on-board systems in detail, offering information and options and providing a framework for owners of sailboats, from small bay cruisers to larger ocean-sailing yachts, in order to help you to make decisions and begin actual projects. Our hope is that our experience and research will help you in several ways—to fit your boat out in Bristol fashion, to enjoy cruising and sailing more with family and friends and to protect the value of your boat.

# Chapter One

# SAIL HANDLING SIMPLIFIED

*How to set up sailing systems to get the best results.*

- ▲ Setting Up Conventional Rigs
- ▲ Conventional Mainsail Options
- ▲ Conventional Mainsail Running Systems
- ▲ Conventional Headsail Systems
- ▲ Roller Furling-Reefing Headsails
- ▲ Roller Furling-Reefing Mainsails
- ▲ Downwind Sails and Systems
- ▲ Fully Automated Sailing Systems

The history of sailing is the history of designers and seafarers striving to make sail handling easier and more efficient. The development of the fore-and-aft rig was a huge development in the 1800s. The Bermudian rig, which became popular in the 1920s, was another giant stride forward. However, in the last twenty years there have been dozens of advances tailored to the needs of recreational- and offshore-cruising sailors. Handling sails today is much easier than it was just twenty years ago, and as a result the size of boats manageable by a small crew has increased enormously. It is not unusual to find a middle-aged couple handling a 20-ton, 50-footer all by themselves, with the aid of all manner of labor-saving devices. Increased size often means increased comfort and speed, which in turn add to the fun of spending time on the water. In this chapter we will describe the advances and innovations in rigs and sails that have made this possible.

When you contemplate how you want to rig a new boat or how best to change and upgrade the existing rig on your boat, you have to consider both the standing and the running rigs. The standing rig comprises the masts and booms and the fixed-wire rigging holding them aloft, while the running rigging is the sails, as well as all the halyards, sheets and downhauls you use to hoist and trim the sails. Whether you plan to sail with the latest in sail-handling gear and high-tech equipment and instruments or with a simple and standard rig, you will have to think of how you want to set up the mast so that it does what you need it to do, and how to arrange the sails so that they perform to their best. To do this, it is best to think of the whole rig as two interrelated systems.

*The standing rig:* In general the standing rig must be set up in such a way that it keeps the mast or masts vertical, stationary and unbent under the pressures of sailing. Moreover the standing rig ought to be adjustable to the point that sail trim can be affected, either temporarily or permanently. The standing rig should not be simply set up at launching time and then forgotten. Wire stretches, boats change shape slightly, and sails require different amounts of rake or mast bend. The standing rig is dynamic and requires thought and trim just like the sails and running rig. How you plan to sail and what type of running rigging you plan to use will affect how you set up and adjust your standing rig.

*The running rig:* There are so many ways to approach the running rig that most sailors design their own combination of systems to get the overall sailing system they need and want. In general the running rig should be arranged to suit the boat's normal crew, should be simple enough to work in both very light and heavy weather, should be as adjustable or tweakable as possible and should include the right sails for any wind strength or wind direction you are likely to meet. How you decide to set up the running rig will in most cases depend upon your sailing experience—whether you prefer to sail with many guys, downhauls and so forth or without them.

As we discuss the wide variety of rigs and sail-handling systems available to sailors, both the standing and the running rigs for each system will be covered so that the relationship between the two can be understood. The aim of this chapter is to help both newcomers and experienced sailors simplify sail handling and make the best of the available techniques and equipment. My biases are clear: I like roller-furling/roller-reefing sails, having sailed many thousands of miles with them; I like spinnakers, mizzen staysails and other fun and fast sails; and I like a rig with enough sail combinations to allow the boat to be sailed efficiently in everything from 5 knots to 40 knots. That said, I have owned and sailed just about all conventional and modern rigs and know that each system has its benefits and its drawbacks.

Setting up the right sailing system for you and your boat requires almost a statement of personal philosophy: Are you a traditionalist or a pragmatist or a futurist? Whichever you are, there's a rig for you.

## SETTING UP CONVENTIONAL RIGS

Most boats today are rigged with a straightforward Bermudian sloop arrangement. The days of gaff-headed rigs are gone, and in boats under 45 feet it is rare today to see a yawl or a ketch. The standard production sloop, as we know it, has evolved from boats designed for performance around the racecourse. Yet there are other strong influences as well: the bareboat charter business has contributed many design features to today's boats, including the wide acceptance of roller-furling headsails; and traditional work boat design, full keels, short rigs and so forth have contributed to the development of conservative blue-water passagemakers.

Still, today's sailboat, more often than not, is a fiberglass sloop, with a fairly high aspect (tall) mainsail with some roach curve and partial battens and, forward, a standard 120 percent genoa hanked onto the headstay with piston hooks. Most manufacturers of new boats offer roller-furling headsails as an option and many buyers opt for them. But, for those who choose not to and for all those who sail older boats that have not been retrofitted with roller headsails, there

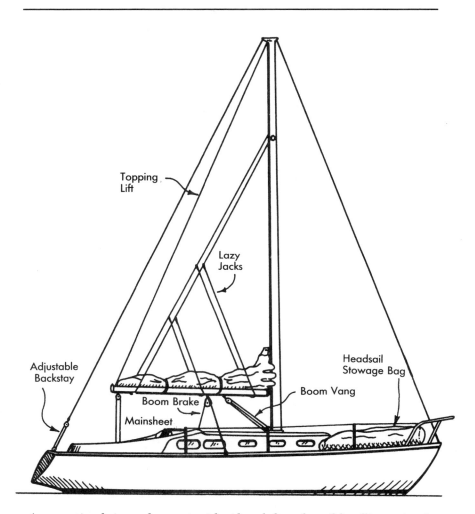

*A conventional rig can be set up with aids to help make sail handling easier: lazy jacks, boom brake, boom vang, adjustable backstay, deck stowage bag for the head-sail.*

are a several important points to think of when setting up the standing and running rig.

The first item of business is to make sure the standing rig is set up correctly and is adjusted for your sails and sailing style. The object of setting up the rig is to ensure, first, that it stays standing in all conditions and, second, that it helps you trim your sails effectively. The mast should be set up in tension: all stays—lowers, caps shrouds, headstay and backstay—are tight, the mast is centered over the hull and the headstay is tauter than the rest to prevent sagging.

It is common practice to set up a masthead sloop that is not fitted with hydraulics on the backstay with a slight prebend in the mast. The bend back at the top of the mast is achieved by setting the mast up centered and straight first. Then gradually tighten the backstay until the top one third of the mast curves slightly aft. Prebend sets the rig up for a wide range of sailing conditions, gives you a good indication of the tension in the rig and, most importantly, ensures that you do not bend the mast forward when sailing to windward. Masts fail when they bend out of column because the cap shrouds are too loose or because they bend forward above the spreaders when the backstay is too loose.

If you have an adjustable or hydraulic backstay, you will be able to tune the tension in the rig by fine increments. As you sail upwind in a rising breeze, you increase tension on the backstay, thereby keeping the headstay bar taut and putting a slight backward curve in the top of the mast, which flattens out the mainsail and moves the main's draft forward. As you head off the wind or as the wind drops, you can decrease tension on the backstay to give more shape to the main and relax tension on the headstay. At the end of the day you can further decrease tension on the backstay, giving all the swagings, turnbuckles and fittings on the fore and backstays a rest. You will find that an hydraulic or easily adjustable backstay will significantly improve the windward performance of your boat.

Tension meters are available to measure the approximate tension of the stays as you set up the rig. The simplest is the Loos Tension Meter, available through most catalog houses and chandleries. Such meters are most useful on smaller boats with smaller stay-wire sizes. On larger boats, unless you plan to install complex and expensive strain gauges, it is necessary to develop a "feel" for stay tension and to continually watch how stays stretch.

The single most common failure point in the standing rig is at the rolled swagings that form the terminals on most rigs. The wire (1-by-19 stainless steel) is compressed within the swaging under great loads. Yet the swaging itself is open at the wire end, permitting water to percolate down the wire into the interior of the swaging. Even though all the parts are stainless steel, corrosion can form, which in time can break wire stands where they emerge from the swaging. In extreme cases the swaging itself can crack. In either case once the stainless has begun to fail, you must replace the whole stay. Stainless steel has the bad habit of looking fine until it fails completely.

A quick word about stainless steel: Although 316-grade stainless steel is used by all reputable rigging and gear manufacturers as a minimum grade, the steel is only stainless while it can react with air. When stainless steel is immersed in water and cut off from air (inside a swaging), the stainless properties of the alloy cease to work. Hence the corrosion. To prevent corrosion the open ends of all swagings should be filled with silicone and checked and refilled with silicone on a regular basis.

The best terminals for standing wire rigging are Norseman or StaLok fittings. These are patented mechanical terminals, which can be assembled and disassembled by anyone and can be replaced if suspect. Experienced ocean sailors prefer these terminals because they can be checked, repaired and adapted to repairs. Also, unlike swagings, mechanical terminals are not subject to interior corrosion. But they are much more expensive than swagings.

Rod rigging, which is used on most racing boats and many high-tech cruising boats, has the advantage over 1-by-19 wire of greater strength for its weight, lower windage and less stretch. Manufacturers such as Navtec have perfected the terminal fittings and spreader-end fittings that once were a source of failure in rod rigs. The new systems of rod rigging are comprised of discontinuous sections that terminate in special tip cups at the ends of the spreaders as well as at the mast and on deck. If you choose to go with rod rigging, you will find it more expensive than wire, but it offers better performance. If you want to upgrade your rig to a high level of performance, rod rigging with an adjustable hydraulic backstay should be your choice.

For those with older boats the question of a rig's useful life-span needs answering. Rigs that are well maintained, used seasonally and unstepped during the off season last ten years on average. If the rig is stored inside and is maintained by a professional rigger, that life-span will increase to twelve to fifteen years or longer. Rigs that are left stepped year-round, whether sailed or not, will last a somewhat shorter time—eight years on average. Lastly, rigs that are used actively for offshore sailing and are left standing year-round will have a useful life-span of five to eight years.

If your rig is getting old or if you are looking at purchasing an older boat with its original rig, you may have to consider rerigging the boat.

Each owner will have his preference how the rig should be upgraded, but in general, cruising sailors will seek the durability and elasticity of wire, whereas racers and "performance" cruisers will seek the low windage and low stretch of rod. For those choosing to rerig with wire, it is wise to use mechanical Norseman or StaLok end fittings if possible. In either case, to do the rerigging job correctly, you should include an hydraulic backstay adjuster, replace tangs on the mast, turnbuckles and toggles at the deck and include radio insulators in the backstay.

The cost of such an upgrade using 1-by-19 stainless-steel wire and undertaken by a professional rigger will run approximately $150 per foot of mast, or $6,000 for a 40-foot mast (circa 1991). Doing the job yourself will save you 20 percent or more. Rod rigging should only be installed by a professional and will cost approximately 30 percent more than wire.

## CONVENTIONAL MAINSAIL OPTIONS

Although the world of sailing has moved rapidly in the past few years to find new ways to handle and set up sailing and running rigs, there are still many virtues in the conventional, low-tech systems. First, sails that travel on their own slides up and down the mast or headstay can always be taken down. Second, conventional gear is low-tech enough for almost any sailor to be able to effect repairs of his sails and running rig—even at sea. And, lastly, setting up a conventional rig is the least expensive way to get a cruising boat away from the dock and under sail.

The Bermudian rig—masthead or fractional sloop—that is so common today has evolved over seventy years to a highly refined degree, and many tricks, techniques and innovations have been developed to make sail handling easier and more efficient.

The mainsail is the workhorse and largest working sail in the rig. The standard sail offered by sailmakers today will be Dacron with two sets of reef points for slab of "jiffy" reefing and will have a slightly rounded roach supported by three or four battens. This sail has evolved from racing sails, which in turn were developed to get the most unpenalized sail area under a given racing rule while providing a straight trailing edge. For cruising purposes the partially battened main should be considered only one of the possible options.

Mainsails for coastal and offshore cruising boats should be built to last and to perform in a wide range of conditions—0 to 40 knots. Most cruising sailors will not carry two mains—even circumnavigators. If you are having a mainsail made, decide what type of sail you need and then seek out a sailmaker with experience building that type of sail. Your local sailmaker who has always done your repairs and is a jack of all trades may well have overlooked the advances in his trade. Be sure your sailmaker will give you triple stitching and will hand-sew the headboard, will include webbing for strength at the clew and tack and will add a third reef point. The sail should be serviceable in winds ranging from 0 to 40 knots, which means heavy cloth, robust construction and attention to detail. On partially battened sails be sure the batten pockets are reinforced at both ends and that there is a mechanical way—either stitching or a small bolt—to hold the batten in the pocket.

Two other types of mainsails have found favor among cruising sailors who had found the partially battened mainsail to be inefficient and subject to hard spots in the sail where the battens end. The fully battened main, long outlawed by racing-rule makers, has found loyal followings among multihull sailors, board sailors and even some traditional racing sailors. And the roachless, battenless main has found a following among those who are willing to sacrifice sail area aloft and a small fraction of their boat's performance for durability, ease of handling and cost savings.

Of the three types of mainsails, the partially battened sail is the most common, as such sails are more often than not supplied with a boat when prepared for sail by a manufacturer or dealer. Yet if you are upgrading your rig-and-sail complement, you may well want to exchange your partially battened mainsail for fully battened one. Retrofitting an existing sail is not too expensive—approximately $750 for a 600-square-foot sail. If you are having a new main built, having it made with full battens will increase the cost. But the extra costs will more than pay for themselves in the added life full battens give a sail.

There are many benefits to using full battens. The sail will be quieter and more docile when it is luffed, tacked and jibed. You will be able to add roach to the sail and give yourself more sail area. The fully battened sail holds its shape better in both light and heavier winds and can be shaped more consistently with backstay bend, halyard, and foot tension and leech-chord adjustments. And when dropping the sail, a fully battened main dropped into lazy jacks on the boom will furl itself neatly and quickly. Your boat will sail faster and will be easier to sail with a full battened mainsail than with a partially battened sail.

The single significant drawback to full-battened sails is the increased chafe on the sail. If you have a conventionally stayed mast, with fore and aft lowers, you will find that when sailing off the wind, the lower battens are in constant contact with the aft lower shroud. In just a matter of days of downwind sailing, the shroud will chafe through the batten pocket and sail. The cure is to add chafe strips to the sail and to apply chafe gear—tape, plastic shroud covering, even baggy wrinkle—to the lower shrouds.

Fully battened sails also tend to chafe at the sail's luff, where batten pockets rub against the mast as well as absorbing all the compression load of the batten as the sail fills. In a retrofit of full battens to an existing sail, the simplest way to guard against chafe at the mast is to sew sections of nylon webbing, or elk hide, over the end of the pocket. While chafe will still eventually wear through, such robust material will last for years before needing renewal.

For new sails Harken and other gear manufacturers have developed batten end fittings that double as slide cars. The cars run either up a section of traveler track fitted to the aft side of the mast or can be fitted with nylon slugs, which will run up the existing slug-slot in the mast. Either way the batten end fittings protect the batten pocket from damage, while proving a sturdy car for hoisting the sail. The Harken solution is costly when compared with simple track slides. But when you add up the expected extra life of the sail, along with the ease of handling provided by the cars, you may feel the investment has been worthwhile.

The battenless main, which has come into vogue as sailors have accepted the in-mast roller-furling main systems made popular by Hood Yacht Systems and others, has long been used by voyaging sailors more interested in simplicity than high performance. The advantages of a battenless main are its low cost, small relative size, hence ease of handling, and its low maintenance.

Yet unless you have a roller main, which we will discuss later, the roachless, battenless main may not offer the performance most modern sailors demand. Sailing to windward, it is difficult to trim an efficient air-foil shape into a battenless main, and when the wind pipes up, it is difficult to adjust the sail's draft with mast bend and halyard tension.

If you seek the simplicity of a battenless main, it makes sense, then, to set the sail free-footed, with only an adjustable outhaul at the sail's

*Fully battened mains provide more power, but they can be harder to raise and lower. One solution is the sliding traveler car running on a track attached to the mast. Harken has come up with an off-the-shelf system called the Battcar. (Courtesy Harken.)*

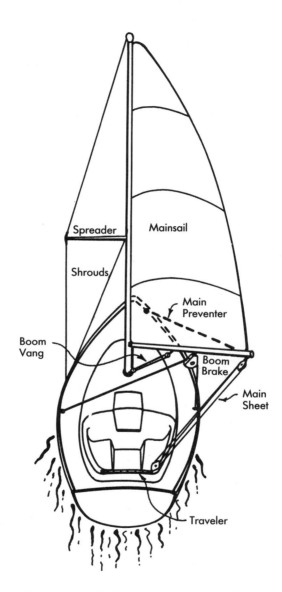

Spreader

Mainsail

Shrouds

Main
Preventer

Boom
Vang

Boom
Brake

Main
Sheet

Traveler

*The mainsail can be best controlled with the mainsheet, plus a boom vang, boom brake or adjustable vangs, and the preventer from the boom's end.*

clew. The sail itself should be cut with a full shape, particularly in the skirt of the foot, that can then be flattened with foot and halyard tension. Gaining enough twist with a fair trailing edge on the sail is a problem with a battenless main, particularly in lighter breezes with the wind forward of the beam. One simple trick is to move the main traveler to windward and ease or tighten foot tension until you have created an efficient foil. An overtrimmed, sheeted-down, flattened battenless mainsail will stop your boat like a bucket off the stern.

## CONVENTIONAL MAINSAIL RUNNING SYSTEMS

There are four things you want to be able to do easily and well with your main: trim it, reef it, control the main boom and furl it. Since the main is a big sail, you need carefully to rig the lines and systems that you use to control it and you need to use line that is long enough and strong enough.

Trimming the main is a skill that can take time to acquire. The shape of the sail will vary on various points of sail and will show different degrees of efficiency. In general the main should be trimmed by letting it out until it luffs and then trimming it in again. However, with fully battened sails you'll find that the main won't luff until it is backwinded by the genoa, so the trim point will be in somewhat from the luff point. Trial and error and telltales on the trailing edge of the battens will have to be your guides. The second test for trim is to maneuver the sheet until the top batten—on partially battened sails— is parallel to the boom. If you have telltales on the leech, these should be flying straight out backward. In lighter airs you will want to trim in more twist to the sail. As the breeze freshens, you will want to flatten the sail and depower it by sheeting it farther to leeward.

A boom vang is considered essential equipment on racing boats, and rigid boom vangs such as Hall Spars's QuickVang have become increasingly popular on cruising boats. The vang flattens the sail, doubles as a topping lift for the boom, and controls the boom. When linked with the adjustments of the halyards, mainsheet and traveler, the vang gives you the last iota of sail-shape control.

For running downwind a preventer is useful. Rigged from the end of the boom and sheeted forward, the preventer stops the main from

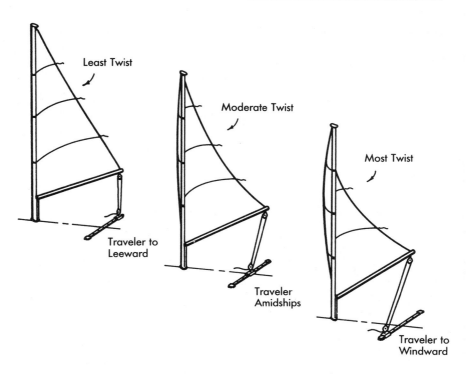

*Trimming a main requires putting in or taking out the right amount of twist. More wind, less twist. Less wind, more twist. Use the traveler and vang tension to get the telltales streaming straight aft.*

swinging through an accidental all-standing jibe. The preventer line can be simply a long guy line that is tied to the end of the boom and then made fast forward. On some offshore boats you will see such a line fixed permanently, with the line coiled and hanging from the forward end of the boom when not in use. Another approach is to use a vang tackle—a three-part piece with shackles at both ends— attached to the middle of the boom and to the toe rail near the turn-buckles for the upper shrouds. It makes sense with such a tackle to have the line long enough to lead back to the cockpit for trimming. Yet another approach is to mount two vang tackles, port and starboard, and simply leave them rigged while out sailing. The two tackles can be used to adjust the position of the boom, to vang the sail, and to act as preventers. Although the double vang–tackle system requires a lot of line spaghetti on deck, it is a simple and efficient way to control the main and boom. Finally, the job of controlling the boom and preventing sudden jibes can be handled by the Dutchman Boom Brake, which is a patented device that fits to the underside of the boom and is controlled and trimmed with lines led on both side decks to the cockpit. Philippe Jeantot used this brake during the first BOC Round The World Race and proved its efficiency and usefulness.

Reefing the main should be a painless job, accomplished quickly. Otherwise the job of reefing will be put off until the wind has risen, making the job more difficult. Almost all cruising boats with conventional rigs have slab or jiffy reefing. The old roller-reefing mains, with round booms and all the attendant trim problems, are things of the past. If you have a roller boom, the best thing to do is to convert it to slab reefing with the addition of two reef points in the sail and cheek blocks and cleats on the boom. You'll be surprised at the increase in performance.

It is standard on slab-reefing systems to have both the main halyard and the reefing lines leading to the mainmast. While it means making a trip out of the cockpit in rough weather, I prefer the simplicity of this system. On *Clover* I can release the mainsheet, move forward, release the halyard and hook the next reef cringle, rehoist the main and haul in the reefing line on the reefing winch in less time than it takes to type this sentence. To simplify the job, it is helpful to mark the main halyard with sail-thread whippings or Magic Marker at the correct point for each reef.

But many sailors prefer to remain in the cockpit and shun the foredeck in deteriorating weather. Who can blame them? For these sailors, single-line reefing systems have been developed in which the main halyard and the reefing lines are led aft to the cockpit. Harken has developed an off-the-shelf system that can be fitted easily to most rigs. The Harken system has been tested extensively by boatbuilders such as Hinckley, who have done a lot of work of their own to make sail handling and reefing easier. Or you may decide to fit a system yourself. To fit such a system on your existing boom, you will need to replace your reefing line with a line long enough to run through the sail and back to the cockpit. Below the boom fix two turning blocks, either on the mast or on deck, to accept the reefing line and a new line that leads back up the mast, through the first reef tack cringle and back down the other side of the sail to a cleat or eye fastened to the mast well below the boom. The two lines—reef and tack lines—are then joined aft of their turning blocks—with shackles,

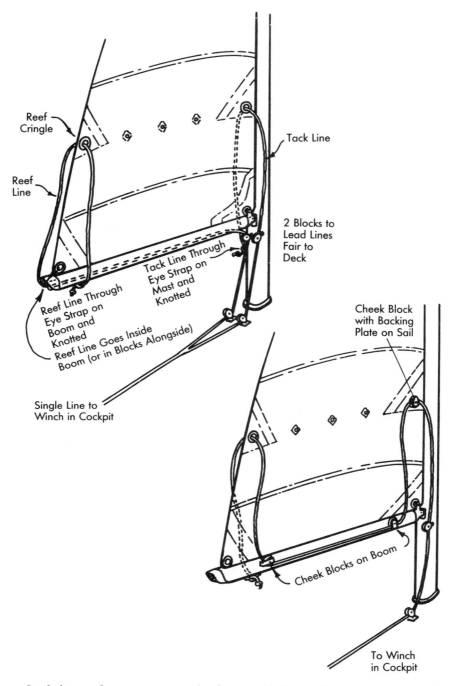

Reef Cringle

Reef Line

Tack Line

2 Blocks to Lead Lines Fair to Deck

Tack Line Through Eye Strap on Mast and Knotted

Reef Line Through Eye Strap on Boom and Knotted

Reef Line Goes Inside Boom (or in Blocks Alongside)

Single Line to Winch in Cockpit

Cheek Block with Backing Plate on Sail

Cheek Blocks on Boom

To Winch in Cockpit

*Single-line reefing systems can either be assembled yourself or you can use an off-the-shelf system. When rigging the lines, adjust the lengths so that the clew and tack both come firmly down to the boom.*

splices or bowlines—and led aft to a winch. Hauling in on the single line tightens the tack and clew of the sail simultaneously. You will have to play with line length before you get them exactly right. The clew line will probably require about a foot more tension than the tack. While it is possible to rig all three reef points in this fashion—or in one of the other single-line systems developed by sailmakers and riggers—you will find your mast and cabin top becoming a spider web of lines. Lastly there is a lot of friction in single-line systems, so you will need a large winch to make it operate smoothly and will have to watch your lines for chafe.

Furling a conventional mainsail with a small crew has always been a problem, for the sail falls all over the deck and you need three hands to control it while you try to secure it to the boom with sail ties. That's why the development of lazy jacks came right after the invention of the fore-and-aft sailing rig three hundred years ago. For dousing and furling a mainsail nothing helps more than lazy jacks.

Simple systems can be rigged with nothing more than line and a few fair leads. It is best on larger boats to have three falls to the boom, while on smaller boats you can get away with only two. There are off-the-shelf systems available from Harken and others that are well engineered and simple to install. Whether you choose to fit your own design or a store-bought version, it is important to be able to tighten and loosen the lazy jacks easily. You will find that permanently rigged jacks can be a nuisance when hoisting the main. Battens tend to catch under the lines. Also, you need to be able to unrig the lazy jacks when you rig an over-the-boom awning.

There are several other systems that have been developed to assist in furling and stowing mains. The Zip-Stop system is a device that fits on the aft side of the mainmast and collects the main into a zippered pouch as it furls the sail. The Doyle StackPack system controls the sail with lazy jacks and then furls the sail within a sewn-on acrylic pouch at the foot of the sail. And the Dutchman system controls the sail while it is lowered with vertical guy lines fixed between the boom and the topping lift and threaded through grommets in the sail; when the halyard is let go, the sail flakes itself along the guy lines atop the boom. All three systems have eased handling of the big mainsail and have made sailing a bit easier and safer.

Conventional mainsails and running systems have evolved over the years to a high degree. For those setting out to design a new system

*Lazy jacks make dropping the main much easier. On larger boats a three-fall system as shown above will catch the whole length of the sail. If the sail is luffing when it is dropped, it will fall nearly flaked on top of the boom.*

or upgrade an older boat with a new mainsail system, there are plenty of options. My choice for a complete conventional system is: full battens, lazy jacks, a rigid boom vang such as the QuickVang, a Dutchman Boom Brake and a prerigged preventer.

# CONVENTIONAL HEADSAIL SYSTEMS

It is common for sailors using conventional headsails to carry a minimum of two sails—genoa and jib—for light and heavy conditions. However, a well-dressed cruising boat should carry at least four headsails, not including spinnakers. These should be: a 130 to 150 percent genoa for winds up to 15 knots or so; a 100 to 120 percent working genoa for winds of 15 to 25 knots; a 75 to 85 percent high-cut working jib (or Yankee) for winds up to 35 knots or so; and a spitfire storm jib.

With all of these sails on board it becomes a task to stow them effectively when not in use and then to arrange those in use on the foredeck so that they can be hoisted, trimmed and dropped with a minimum of fuss.

The effectiveness of your headsails will depend to a large degree on the tightness of your headstay. A sagging stay will decrease the headsail's windward performance and will put additional strain on the mast. Setting up the headstay properly entails adjusting the headstay and inner stays, such as a forestay and baby stay, so that the mast is either vertical or has a slight prebend aft. Once this is done, you increase headstay tension by tightening the backstay. If you have an hydraulic or mechanical backstay adjuster as described above, you will find that you can crank in more tension when going to windward and therefore greatly increase the performance of your headsails.

Remember, the headstay will have to stand up to a lot of strain, a lot of jarring motion and a lot of vibration. It should be the heaviest stay on the boat—one size larger than the cap shrouds and backstay—and needs to be fitted with toggles at both ends to ensure that vibration does not cause stress fractures in the wire and swaging.

On most boats the headsail sheets will lead aft through blocks or adjustable sheet cars mounted on tracks. These create the angle of trim for the sail and need to be adjusted as the wind increases or decreases. To decrease the twist in the headsail or depower it as the wind picks up, move the sheet car aft. To increase the twist and close the slot between the headsail's leech and the mainsail as the wind decreases, the car should be slid forward. Additionally as you change headsails, shortening down from the number one to number two and

*When changing to a smaller headsail, the sheet car needs to be moved forward. The simple system shown on the Jeanneau sloop above permits you to haul the sheet car forward to the new position. When a larger sail is put on again, the natural pressure on the car will force it aft, where it can be made fast with the trim line through the jam cleat. This system works well for roller-furling headsails too.*

finally number three, you will need to adjust the cars again. To get the best from your headsail trim, establish the various car settings for each sail and mark these with Magic Marker or small brass or plastic plaques so you can immediately go to the correct setting.

The tack fitting for the headsails should be a heavy snap shackle with a lanyard on the pull ring. If you anticipate frequent sail changes, you will want to set up two snap shackles at the stem head so you can hank on a second sail while the first is still flying.

Not all boats are fitted with two jib halyards. Yet it is prudent to have a spare halyard ready to go. If possible, it is wise to add a second halyard, either by reeving one internally or, if necessary, by adding an external halyard. Halyards can be either rope-wire or all rope. On a rope-wire halyard the wire needs to be long enough to lead from the head of the sail, through the sheave at the masthead, and down to the halyard winch, where it should make at least four turns. Ideally the splice will fall between the winch and the cleat, where it will not be under strain, nor will it be twisted on the winch or cleat. For sails with shorter luffs, use a wire pennant to make up the difference in length. Modern Kevlar-cored lines have such low stretch that they are often preferred to wire halyards because they are easy on your hands, do not get "meat-hooks" (broken wire strands) that can rip sails and skin and because they do not chafe against the mast, spreaders and other rigging. Also, rope halyards do not require the difficult and expensive wire-rope splice, which is normally done by a professional rigger. If you choose all-rope halyards, make certain the brand and style are rated for the job at hand. In addition, even small halyards need to be of a size that are easy on your hands. For reliability and comfort, ⅜-inch line should be considered a minimum, and ⁷⁄₁₆- or ½-inch is much better.

Shackles on headsails are often the failure points. Snap shackles are commonly used, yet these have the bad habit of flying open when the sail is luffing in rising wind. Be sure the shackle is in good condition—not bent or badly corroded—and that the pin slides firmly into place when attached. If you intend to leave the sail hoisted for a passage, taping the shackle closed can save a lot of hassle. Conservative sailors will opt for D-shackles or dedicated halyard screw shackles such as those made by Wichard and Schaefer Marine.

On wire halyards the shackle will normally be fastened with a Nicopress fitting. These are reliable but need to be inspected regularly to ensure that the press is holding the eye firmly in place and that the shackle is not chafing unduly. On rope halyards experienced sailors often opt to attach shackles with a bowline instead of a splice. A bowline can be untied easily to replace a worn or bent shackle. Moreover, unlike a tapered splice, a bowline will not jam in a sheave at the top of the mast. If you choose to use a spliced end on your halyard, you should put a stopper ball on the line to prevent the splice from entering the sheave.

The most difficult task involved in flying a headsail is getting a large sail down in a rising wind. There are several ways to make this job easier. First, of course, it makes sense to reduce sail before it becomes absolutely necessary. But, given that the sail will be unruly when it is coming down, it is helpful to have sail ties ready to secure it as soon as it comes on deck. These can be looped through the stanchion bases on both sides of the foredeck.

When changing down to a smaller headsail, it helps to lay the new headsail on the windward deck and secure it with sail ties. Attach the tack to the spare tack shackle and the piston hanks to the headstay, removing the lowest hanks on the genoa if necessary. The jib is now secure and ready to go.

When ready to drop the big sail, head the boat off, blanket the sail with the mainsail, and drop the genoa onto the leeward deck. You can then secure it with sail ties before removing the hanks from the headstay. This done, the halyard and sheets can be swapped to the jib, the sheet cars can be moved forward and then the jib can be hoisted. Again, this is easier to do if the sail is in the lee of the main. If you are beating to windward, you can pretrim the jib while it is blanketed and avoid the grunt work of grinding in the sheet with the wind working against you.

Furling headsails on deck is neither good for the sails nor good for mobility around the foredeck. Instead, an unused headsail can be flaked on deck and then furled and made fast along the lifelines. The sail ties need to be made fast halfway up the stanchions, and the sail's clew needs to be folded forward on itself before the sail can be put away. It is important to get the sail off the deck to allow boarding waves to wash through without taking the genoa with it. Naturally, in rough conditions the sail will have to be bagged and moved aft to ensure that it stays aboard.

Stowing sails on the foredeck while at anchor, or while a different sail is being used, often results in a pile of sail bags tied to handrails forward of the mast. A better solution is to have sail covers sewn for one or two headsails that can be furled and stowed along the lifelines. A sail cover can be constructed to fasten to the top lifelines and to the stanchions forward of the mast. Permanent sail ties should be fixed inside the sail cover into which the sail can be furled. Once tied down firmly, the sail cover is wrapped around the sail and closed with a full-length zipper. Such sail covers can be rigged on either side of the bow, should you want to have your genoa and working jib ready to fly.

There are several other "labor-saving" devices that have been promoted for handling headsails. The downhaul, which is a line rigged up the luff of the sail and used to haul down the sail, can be of some help. Yet a downhaul is only really suited to sails flying from bowsprits. On conventional modern sloops such a rig is rarely needed and clutters the deck with unnecessary line and blocks.

A reefing headsail is another improvement that may be more trouble than it is worth. While it may seem attractive to have a single working jib that can be lowered and reefed by a third, such a sail is very difficult to build and cannot be as efficient as a second smaller sail. Moreover, the tack and clew of a reefed headsail will have to be so heavily built that they will detract from the performance of the sail when fully set. Lastly, in a rising wind the sail will have to be dropped to the deck to tie in new sheets and the reef points, so the labor savings of the sail have been lost. For my money I would always prefer two well-built sails to a single compromise sail.

Setting up a simple and bullet-proof system for handling your conventional headsails will take time as you sort out headstay tension, sheet-car settings and your own reefing and furling procedures. But, given thought and practice, you can take most of the work and pain out of working on the foredeck.

# ROLLER FURLING-REEFING HEADSAILS

Few innovations in sailing systems have been so revolutionary and so widely adopted as roller furling-reefing headsails. Although roller-furling systems have been around for fifty years, it wasn't until the late 1960s that Schaefer Marine reintroduced the concept and marketed aggressively to cruising sailors. In the twenty-five years since,

*Roller furling-reefing headsails make sailing easier and more fun. While the sail will not have a perfect shape when partially reefed, it will be serviceable reaching and running. A foam luff pad sewn into the sail will add bulk to the belly and flatten the reefed sail for better performance. (Courtesy Harken.)*

dozens of companies have jumped into the market and thousands of sailors have sailed millions of miles with roller-furling gear.

Critics of roller systems make the point that should the system fail, it can be impossible to get your headsail down. That may be true. However, once a sailor has become familiar with roller-furling equipment, he will find that it is virtually trouble-free. The great sailing test ground for cruising gear is the BOC Singlehanded Round The World Race, run every four years. Since the inaugural race in 1982, 90 percent of the boats to compete in the event have used roller gear for their headsails. In the vast majority of the cases the sailors returned from their 27,000-mile voyages in the deep southern latitudes of the Southern Ocean with their roller gear and sails intact. Most claim they would have been unable to compete in such an event without the gear.

Today more than three quarters of the boats voyaging about the world on extended cruises use roller-furling headsails. Most crews sail great distances shorthanded and find that roller furling makes life under way safer and easier. In my own case, when Rosie and I decided to go off cruising about the world, the first item on our wish list was roller furling for the headsail. I wouldn't cruise without it.

That said, there are several basics to think about when selecting and rigging your boat with roller-furling gear.

All of the best roller-furling gear on the market adapts to an existing headstay by fitting extruded aluminum sections around the stay and a drum around the turnbuckle. The stay itself can be wire or rod. The most important items you may have to add to the headstay when fitting a roller system are toggles at the top and bottom. The stay must have the freedom to move in any direction under load, or the extrusions and the drum fitting can crack.

A second alteration to an existing rig may be a positive screw shackle for the halyard. Most sailors leave their roller jibs hoisted for the entire season, although it is kind to the sail to relax halyard tension when not under way. With the shackle out of sight and out of mind for that long, you should take the precaution of replacing the snap shackle with a more robust model.

Choosing a roller unit will involve personal choices regarding manufacturers, price and how you intend to use the unit. Schaefer Marine was the first company to move into the market. But they did so with a luff-wire system that did not fit around the headstay and therefore had very poor luff tension. It was only in 1989 that Schaefer brought out their extruded aluminum model for fitting around the headstay. The models offered by Schaefer are extremely well engineered, although to date they have not had as much sea time as some other models. Hood Yacht Systems and Harken have established themselves as the leaders in the U.S. market for roller-furling gear. Hood has long been an innovator in roller technology; they are called upon now to build systems for every type of boat, from 12-foot day sailers to 120-foot megayachts.

Harken has been in the market for many years as well with a superbly engineered system that rolls on very smooth plastic ball bearings. The Harken systems have raced and cruised all over the world with success, and many offshore sailors and riggers swear by the system.

Both the Hood SeaFurl and the Harken system fit over the headstay and include an integral turnbuckle. A retrofit on an existing rig requires the headstay to be cut and a new mechanical end fitting (StaLok or Norseman) applied so that the turnbuckle-drum attachment can be fitted. The advantages of such a setup is the ability to adjust headstay tension without removing or adjusting the roller drum. When Mike Plant chose the Harken system for his 1990 BOC racer *Duracell,* he cited this as one of his main reasons.

ProFurl, a French system, produces roller-furling systems that fall in the same category as the Harken and Hood models, although slightly more expensive. Unlike the American systems, however, the ProFurl can be fitted over an existing turnbuckle. This means you must remove the drum to adjust the forestay. But a benefit is the additional strength provided by the stainless-steel straps that support the roller unit—a belt-and-braces solution. The ProFurl bearings are steel and sealed in a watertight compartment, while both Hood and Harken have plastic bearings in unsealed compartments. The advantage of the American systems is the ability to flush them with fresh water and inspect them from time to time. On the other hand, ProFurl's steel bearings will bear up under a significantly greater side loading—when reefing the sail in strong winds—than will plastic bearings, which distort if put under extreme loads. Since a headsail should never be reefed while still full and under maximum load, this bearing distortion rarely becomes a problem.

At the lower end of the price scale are retrofit units from companies such as Cruising Designs and the Hood SeaFurl LD. These are good units that will serve coastal cruisers well and can be fitted to just about any boat. The key to long service with these and other units is to keep them flushed with fresh water to prevent corrosion and to refrain from cranking in reefs—partial rolls—when the sail is full.

At the high-tech end of the scale you will find electrically and hydraulically operated units manufactured by Hood, ProFurl and by the German manufacturer Reckman. On boats of 50 feet and up, with working genoas of 750 square feet or more, a mechanical assist while reefing or furling the headsail can be most welcome. For those who like redundancies on their automated gear, look for manual overrides for winding up the headsail in the event that the electrical or hydraulic system fails.

The headsails you will use on your roller furling should be tailored to the purpose. In general it is good to carry two headsails, a genoa of 125 percent or so for coastal sailing, and a working headsail of 85 to 110 percent for offshore work or cruises in windy areas, such as the eastern Caribbean. Your existing headsails can be adapted with luff tapes and can be recut to be slightly flatter for better reefing. In addition, luff pads should be sewn into the luffs of the sails to give them bulk when the sails are rolled up.

If you are having new sails built for a roller furling-reefing system, you should find a sailmaker who has a lot of experience with roller headsails. There are several details in a new headsail that can improve its performance. The sail will need to be slightly higher cut than you might be accustomed to. Yet, a higher-cut sail will roll in and out more easily and will keep its shape better in reefed positions. Additionally, the higher the cut, the more constant will be the sheet-car setting when the sail is reefed.

Instead of using stainless-steel grommets at the head and tack, loops of heavy nylon webbing sewn to the sail will attach it firmly and will keep the sail from bunching around the fittings as it will do around stainless-steel rings. Reinforced corners, with Kevlar patches, can increase the life of the sail, as will nylon-webbing reinforcing at the clew. The sail should be designed to be reefed. Although you will never be able to have a perfect reefed roller headsail, you will find that a fairly flat-cut sail with luff pads sewn in will develop a reasonable shape when reefed about one-third and that shape will improve when reefed two-thirds. A new sail should be marked with clear black stripes running vertically from the foot to show the first and second reefs.

Using roller furling-reefing headsails will make sailing easier and more fun. But there are several simple techniques that you will need to learn to keep yourself out of trouble. First, if you relax the halyard when not in use, remember to tighten it again before going sailing. Failing to do so can create a halyard wrap at the masthead that will lock up the roller system and require someone to go aloft. Some units, such as the ProFurl, have halyard catchers built into the top of the unit to prevent such wraps.

*To keep the sail on a roller-furling device from bunching at the tack and head when the sail is rolled in, remove the stainless-steel grommets and replace them with webbing that will roll flat against the aluminum roller.*

When rolling out the sail, particularly in moderate to strong breezes, be sure to maintain some tension on the roller line as it runs forward and wraps around the drum. The danger is getting an override or a knot on the drum that will tangle the line and prevent you from rolling up the sail later. In heavy weather the furling line should be kept on a winch and the sail partially rolled, thus ensuring that you will be able to get the sail in when necessary.

Running dead downwind presents a potential problem, for should the sail be partially rolled when it is blanketed behind the main, causing it to luff and flutter, it can wrap backward onto itself. The sail can then bind and prevent you from rolling it either in or out. To prevent this, you have to make sure the headsail stays full and does not get blanketed by the main.

When running downwind with the headsail poled out on the spinnaker or whisker pole, you can set the rig up easily while the headsail is furled and then simply roll it out when the topping lift, downhaul and sheet are all in place. Jibing this rig is made simple by again rolling up the headsail, dropping the pole to switch sheets, and then rolling the sail out again. In a rising breeze you can reduce sail to any desired amount and can continue to carry a scrap poled out up to 30 knots of wind or more.

To preserve your roller furling-reefing headsail, make certain the sail is protected from ultraviolet damage with a strip of acrylic cloth along the outside of the leech and foot.

# ROLLER FURLING-REEFING MAINSAILS

Although not yet as widely accepted as roller-furling headsails, roller mains—either in the mast or in the boom—are rapidly developing a wide following. It is easy to see why. When you are sailing along on a pleasant afternoon and the sea breeze begins to build, as it often does along the coast, all you need to do to adjust the size of the main is to roll in a few feet. No rushing forward to the mast to haul down a 30 percent jiffy reef. No luffing of the main when you know you are just slightly overpowered. If all you need to do is roll in 10 inches, then that's what you do. And at the end of the day, when you sail into harbor, you put the sail away for the night with the crank of a winch handle. No flogging sail, no wrestling with stiff sailcloth and no tangle of reefing lines and no sail stops. Magnificent.

Like roller headsails, roller mains—particularly masts and booms from Hood Yacht Systems—have been tested for years and have covered many hundreds of thousands of miles at sea. Dodge Morgan used a roller furling-reefing main during his historic nonstop circumnavigation. Phil Weld used the system during his record-breaking single-handed transatlantic run in the early 1980s. Hundreds of boats have crossed oceans and thousands have cruised extensively with the systems aboard.

In the early years—mid-1970s—in-the-mast furling systems were famous for jamming halfway in as they were being furled in rising winds. This was due to uneven rolls on the internal roller, which forced the sail to jam, usually at the tack. This was remedied by correcting the angle of the boom, and therefore the angle of rolling for the main. Moreover, improved bearings and simplified rolling systems made winding in the big mainsails easier and more efficient.

Also in the early years roller-furling masts had the unpleasant habit of humming like primitive flutes in the wind when the sail was furled. Hood developed a canvas baffle that slips up the slot in the mast to dampen the fluting. And eventually ways were developed to create a mast extrusion with a narrow enough slot to keep it from becoming a musical instrument.

Today there are several different ways to adapt your boat to a roller-furling mainsail. Hood, Z-Spar, Composite Spars and others manufacture masts that are tailor-made for roller mains. To fit such a mast, you need to replace your existing mast and rig, and you may well have to have new chain plates added to the hull. It is far easier to have a new boat fitted with such a complete spar and system, for the designer and builder can optimize the standing rig design and position the mast to offer the best balance.

For those who want to retrofit existing masts with roller mains, there are several different systems that can be adapted to standard aluminum mast extrusions. ProFurl, Facnor (Viscom International) and others have developed systems that can be fitted—in most cases with pop rivets—directly to the mast. In most cases the existing boom can be used as well, with a length of traveler track fitted atop the boom and a traveler car adapted to carry the clew blocks. The furling line can be led through a block at the gooseneck and then back to the cockpit. In most cases the existing mainsheet can be used.

The sail you will use on a roller main is unlike a standard main with fractional battens or full battens. It will have a hollow leech, no battens and a loose foot. It will be smaller and will have less power than a standard main and needs to be trimmed differently.

The sail will be designed to roll easily as well as to sail well, so you will find that it is somewhat flatter in shape than a conventional main. This being the case, you will need to keep an eye on the sail's twist as you trim it and as you roll it in and out. Most mainsheets will have an adjustable traveler, and you will find that to get the best shape to the sail, you will have to trim the traveler to windward, adding twist. Additionally, having a loose foot, you will be able to ease clew tension to give more draft to the sail in lighter winds.

An in-the-mast roller mainsail will never give you the top performance of a fully battened main. Yet the systems that have been developed by Hood and others more than make up for it in convenience and in the pleasures and benefits of incremental sail trim. For those who have never used roller mains, the ability to crank in just the needed amount of sail—10 inches or 10 feet—instead of the 30 percent segments of slab reefs, will actually increase the average sailor's performance.

Yet there are many boat owners and sailors who seek a higher level of performance from their mainsails and a lower investment in mainsail technology. To answer these sailors' needs, Hood and a European manufacturer, SailTainer, have developed in-boom furling systems that can be adapted directly to existing masts and rigs. The Hood StoBoom is a design that evolved over the years from an early attempt that never quite worked. After years of testing and trials the new design does just what it is supposed to do: It offers an infinitely adjustable sail that can have full or partial battens and thus the power and performance to really drive a modern cruising boat.

New to the market in 1989, roller booms may well be the wave of the future. The technology is simpler and less expensive than roller-furling masts, and the performance from the mainsail is better than with either a conventional main or an in-the-mast roller main. For cruising sailors upgrading an existing boat, the roller boom can be a real boon to sailing.

## DOWNWIND SAILS AND SYSTEMS

Although many cruising sailors shun them, spinnakers are the most fun and most effective sails you can carry. The reason so many sailors choose not to carry and fly a spinnaker is the sheer size and power of the sail—and lack of experience with it. Yet there are many systems and rigging tricks that will make life with a spinnaker fulfilling.

There are two choices in downwind sails: the full triradial type of spinnaker or the single-luff, poleless sail. Each has a place on board, and if you can carry both, then do so, because you will find that in

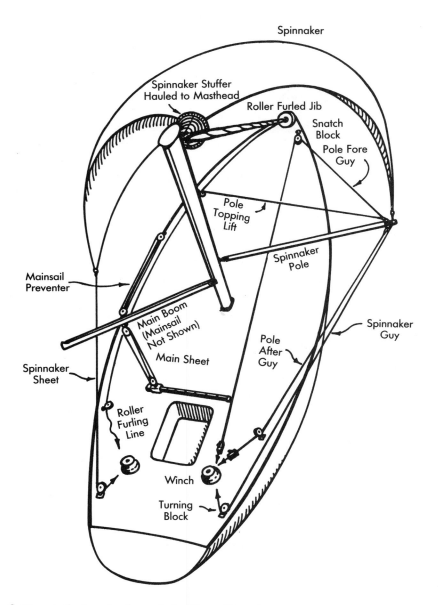

Spinnaker

Spinnaker Stuffer
Hauled to Masthead

Roller Furled Jib

Snatch
Block

Pole Fore
Guy

Pole
Topping
Lift

Spinnaker
Pole

Mainsail
Preventer

Main Boom
(Mainsail
Not Shown)

Main Sheet

Pole
After
Guy

Spinnaker
Guy

Spinnaker
Sheet

Roller
Furling
Line

Winch

Turning
Block

*Setting up the boat for downwind sailing will involve quite a few lines. The systems shown above will enable you to control the main and the spinnaker from the cockpit.*

reaching conditions the single-luff sail will be the better performer while the spinnaker will shine running.

The first challenge to spinnaker sailing is getting the sail up and down without a lot of drama. On boats over 30 feet or so, the best way to do this is with a spinnaker sock or snuffer. There are several commercial brands on the market, but they are not all created equal. By far the best is built by ATN and marketed through Hild and other sailmakers. What makes the ATN snuffer superior is the wide bell opening used at the base. The bell is large enough and fair enough to slide over the spinnaker from the top down—even in strong breezes—without catching and hanging up on a bunch of sailcloth. Additionally the ATN design incorporates an enclosed and endless retrieval line that cannot become tangled in the rigging aloft or twisted up in the roller-furling headsail.

Hoisting and lowering a spinnaker with a snuffer becomes a simple chore. The sail inside the sock should be hoisted in the lee of the mainsail as you run downwind. When the snuffer is pulled to the top of the sail, the spinnaker does not fill suddenly but gives you time to trim it and keep it under control. And when the sail is lowered, the snuffer should be pulled down over the sail while it luffs in the lee of the main. Finally, lower the whole sock to the deck.

The second challenge in spinnaker flying is handling and controlling the spinnaker pole. On larger boats the pole is heavy and unwieldy and on a pitching deck can be a hazard to the crew and the boat. To make the pole easier to handle, you need to rig the standard foreguys and topping lift plus separate afterguys. The foreguy is attached with a snap shackle to the outboard end of the pole and should lead through a block, preferably a snatch block, aft to a winch in the cockpit. The topping lift can run from the end of the pole or from a bridle on the pole. It will be rigged like a halyard; however, if you can run it aft, all the better. A third control line on the pole will add to your comfort on the foredeck. Called an afterguy, the line should run from the cockpit, through a sheet block and to the end of the pole. With this and the foreguy, you can control the pole's position during any maneuver. This is particularly desirable during the takedown in rough seas, when the pole can swing wildly and do damage to the roller-furling extrusion, headstay or your head.

If you are using a spinnaker with a small crew, it is important to learn how to preset the spinnaker sheet (to leeward) and the topping lift and foreguy prior to hoisting the snuffer. Once the halyard has been cleated off, the sock is raised quickly and the spinnaker luffs in the lee of the mainsail until you are ready to trim the guy (windward side) and set up the afterguy on the pole.

The best place to stow and then launch a spinnaker pole is from the forward side of the mast. A track rigged up the mast with an adjustable car enables the pole to be hoisted at its inboard end as the outboard end is made fast on a ring low on the mast. On boats over 40 feet or so you will find that a telescoping pole of the type manufactured by Forespar and also available through Hall Spars will suit your needs better than a solid pole. Remember, a pole on a standard 45-footer will be 20 feet long and will weigh 50 pounds or more. A telescoping pole stowed on the mast can be lowered, led forward, telescoped and rigged with guys and lines without having to lift its full weight at any time.

In rolly conditions, handling a big pole on the foredeck is tricky. It is handy to have sail ties tied on either side of the bow pulpit to lash the pole down while you set up the running rig. Once all the lines are in place, hoist the pole with the topping lift and secure with the foreguys and afterguys.

You will find that a spinnaker trimmed with the pole well aft—squared to the wind—may be harder to keep trimmed and will require more attention than a chute that is trimmed slightly forward. On our passage across the Pacific in *Clover* we used our 1,100-square-foot spinnaker much of the way. We found that when sailing at about 165 degrees apparent and with the chute trimmed somewhat forward and eased on the sheet, the self-steering would steer easily and the sail could go unattended for hours. With a boost of a knot and a half to 2 knots of speed, that was pleasant and fast sailing.

The single luff or cruising spinnaker has become popular in the past decade because it does away with the pole and thus with a lot of the hassle of flying the big sail. Tacked down at the bow, a cruising chute—called a MultiPurpose Sail (MPS), Genniker and other brand names—works well when used with a snuffer such as the ATN. Because it is easier to set up than a spinnaker, you will find that you may use it more often than the bigger, symmetrical sail.

We have found that a cruising chute is best adapted to reaching in light airs. Downwind the sail tends to be blanketed by the main, so it is marginally efficient until you find yourself sailing dead downwind, when you can fly the main and headsail wing-and-wing. However, sailing wing-and-wing, you will have to rig a whisker or spinnaker pole to get the full benefit of the sail's light weight and size.

## FULLY AUTOMATED SAILING SYSTEMS

It used to be that only large and vastly expensive sailing yachts were fitted with automatic systems for hoisting, setting and lowering sails. But in the past few years many innovations have come onto the sailing market aimed at the average cruising sailor who is looking for easier ways to do hard jobs.

*The future of cruising boats might include designs like Procyon. Developed as a research project by Olaf Harken and others, the boat demonstrates that laborsaving gear and new design ideas can work in practice. (Courtesy Harken.)*

The development of small electric and hydraulic winches is what makes automation of even a 35- or 40-footer a practical reality for cruising sailors. Lewmar and Barient have led the way in development of light, high-powered self-tailing winches that will trim your genoa with the press of a button.

On the fully automated cruising boat, the roller headsail is permanently hoisted. The furling line leads to a small electric winch that will reef or furl the sail in just about any conditions. The genoa sheets lead to larger self-tailing winches that can also double as sheet winches for the spinnaker.

The mainsail is a roller furler—either in-the-boom or in-the-mast. The furling line runs through a line stopper to a small electric winch, which in many instances can double as the mainsheet winch.

On larger boats—50 feet and up—main and headsail reefing systems can be installed with their own cranking motors, which can be operated remotely from the cockpit. Such systems, made by Hood, Reckman, ProFurl and others, have the benefit of adding redundancy to the whole operation. Should the motor cranking in the headsail fail, the job can be taken over by a winch in the cockpit driving an emergency furling line.

Lastly, forward at the mast, electric halyard winches, which have to be mounted on deck, assist in hoisting heavy headsails, the spinnaker and the spinnaker pole. These also enable a small person to hoist a very large person up the mast without breaking a sweat.

The choice to be made when considering an automated sailing system is whether to use hydraulics or electricity for cranking power. Both are available from Lewmar, Barient and other companies. Hydraulics require sophisticated engineering and installation. The hydraulic pump will have to be run with electricity, so there will be significant battery drain. However, a hydraulic system suits the marine environment and, once installed and tested, can give reliable service for many years. Electric winches will be less expensive to install and will give excellent service. Although they will draw a lot of amps when in use, draw is sporadic and short. With electric winches you will have to ensure you have enough reserve battery and charging capacity. One benefit of electric winches is the ability to remove the winches easily for servicing.

The fully automated sailing system is not for everyone. But by taking the hard labor out of sailing and by making it possible for smaller people to do heavy jobs, roller-furling equipment and power winches

*Electric roller-furling headsails, such as the ProFurl system, enable a sailor to reef or furl the genoa not only from the cockpit but with the push of a button. Note the winch-handle position on the aft end of the unit. Should the electric motor fail, the sail can be brought in manually.*

can make sailing both safer and more fun. And certainly, as we get longer in the tooth, such labor-saving devices enable us to enjoy sailing longer than we could have in years gone by.

## Further Reading

*Cruising Sails and Rigging,* by Ross Norgrove (Camden, Me.: International Marine Publishing, 1982).

*Offshore Cruising Encyclopedia,* by Steve and Linda Dashew (Ojai, Calif.: Beowulf Publishing Group, 1991).

*Sail Power,* by Wallace Ross (New York: Alfred A. Knopf, 1985).

*Spurr's Boat Book,* by Dan Spurr (Camden, Me.: International Marine Publishing, 1984).

# Chapter Two

# DECK LAYOUTS THAT WORK

*Keep it simple, well organized and uncluttered.*

▲ Sheets, Lines and Halyards

▲ Anchors and Rodes

▲ Big Items: Life Rafts, Windsurfers, Awnings, Etc.

▲ Dinghies and Davits

▲ Cockpit Struts and Arches for Radar, Solar Panels
   and Antennae

I was at the fuel dock in Papeete, Tahiti, early one morning topping up *Clover*'s tanks when the American boat *Y-Not* came alongside the finger pier. It was a 50-footer and crewed by a crowd of young Californians. From the parking lot nearby, one of the crew suddenly appeared at the top of the gangway on a large black motorcycle. He paused and then, with a roar, rode the thing down onto the dock. The others were ready. They had the halyards and straps around the 500-cc bike, and in no time it was in the air and swinging toward the stern. There, aft of the cockpit doghouse, was a large built-in box with its lid thrown open. Into this box the motorcycle was lowered. The lid was screwed shut, and the big toy was secured for the trip to Mooréa, twenty miles away.

*Y-Not* was a unique vessel in many ways. It had been designed around toys as much as any other dictates. There were Windsurfers tucked away in special compartments as well as bicycles, dinghies and surfboards. Yet a real effort had been made to keep the foredeck clear. This was not necessarily for reasons of seamanship. Every evening at about ten o'clock the real reason became apparent as the big deck speakers began to boom and the crew boogied under the bright spreader lights.

It was all a bit of fun, incorporated into the design of a custom boat for a unique individual, reminding me of the T-shirt popular a few years ago emblazoned with the statement HE WHO DIES WITH THE MOST TOYS WINS.

Why not?

Most of us don't take our motorcycles, let alone all our toys, to sea with us. But everyone who sets off cruising with family and friends— even if it is only weekend gunkholing—ends up carrying more than he knows what to do with. It seems inevitable. Our boats are small spaces. Our need for gear, equipment and toys is large. For those heading off to remote regions and across oceans, the need to carry more and more equipment and fuel increases. It is not uncommon in the Pacific to see cruising boats so laden with deck cargo—particularly extra fuel tanks—that people can barely walk on deck.

Experience seems to temper the need to overload an offshore boat. I spoke with American circumnavigator Webb Chiles in Newport, Rhode Island, when he passed through on his *She 36*. The deck of his boat was clear of gear. He commented simply, "Decks shouldn't have any clutter. Keep it simple and sailing will be easier and more fun."

The trick, then, is to organize the deck of your boat to solve several basic problems and to fit the gear and equipment you want within the space available. Deck layouts should improve your ability to handle sails and heavy gear, should arrange for stowage of needed on-deck equipment, should provide useful stowage for toys and should be conceived to minimize clutter.

# SHEETS, LINES AND HALYARDS

The development of singlehanded offshore racing boats for the singlehanded transatlantic race—OSTAR—in the sixties and seventies and for the BOC Singlehanded Round The World Race in the eighties has changed the way we all think about rigging our halyards, lines and sheets. Since most of us cruise shorthanded—two people on 30- to 50-foot boats—many of these innovations are particularly attractive. The trend to bring halyards, uphauls and downhauls aft really caught on in the mid-eighties. The trend has continued to the point that major manufacturers are beginning to incorporate cockpit-led lines into new boats. In 1990 Beneteau introduced a line of designs that take the concept so far that conduits have been molded into the deckhead, permitting halyards and other lines to run aft from the mast to the cockpit unseen and out of the way. Very neat.

The object of arranging your lines, either forward at the mast or aft at the cockpit, is to make sail handling easier for you. The traditional method has long been to have all halyards fall to the base of the mast, to have topping lifts trimmed at the mast, and to lead foreguys for the spinnaker aft to the cockpit. There are a hundred variations on how to set up all of these. However, when thinking about lines at the mast, it is important to link jobs together with the lines you will be needing. For example, when tying in a slab reef, you need to be able to drop the main, fix the new tack cringle, hoist the main again, and tighten the new outhaul for the reef. On *Clover* I do all of this for both the main and the mizzen at the masts. The job of reefing the main requires going forward to the mast, where I'll rarely get wet, and this can be accomplished in under two minutes. The mizzen is reefed at its mast and takes even less time.

To make the job of reefing simple, then, it would make little sense to have the main halyard run aft if you still had to go forward to attach the reefing cringle and haul in the reefing line, only to have to return to the cockpit to rehoist the halyard.

The benefit of leaving all your halyards and other lines led forward at the mast is simplicity. You always go to one place to do a wide variety of jobs. You can look up the mast for tangled halyards and other problems you might miss from the cockpit. And you can drop and gather in sails singlehanded, while paying out the halyard with one hand. But having to go forward to accomplish the smallest task can be a nuisance; it also can be uncomfortable and dangerous in rough weather.

When you decide to reeve lines and halyards aft through turning blocks, you will need to replace those lines with longer ones. On boats with roller-furling headsails and standard mainsails, it makes sense to bring the control lines for the mainsail aft. With only three lines—main halyard, main boom topping lift, and a single-line reefing line (see Chapter One), you will have all necessary lines in the cockpit for handling the mainsail in most conditions. And if you anticipate sailing often in boisterous conditions, you can add a second single-line reefing system to enable a second reef to be taken without leaving the cockpit.

In most cases the lines coming aft will be on top of the cabin house and will terminate on one side of the companionway hatch. Hardware to bring lines aft will include turning sheaves mounted at the base of the mast for each line, plus one or two deck organizers. Ronstan, Schaefer, Harken and others supply a range of low-profile organizers that will route the lines around hatches and Dorade vents to their final destination. In the cockpit these three or four lines can all be handled by one self-tailing winch and good-quality line stoppers. As you design such a system for your own boat, carefully work out the ergonomics. You need to be able to reach each line at the line stopper easily, must be able to flip levers up and down while still controlling a line around the winch, and must be able to stow and sort a lot of line in one small corner of the cockpit.

The line stoppers—Lewmar, Spinlock, Schaefer and others—need to be arranged so that lines feed onto the bottom of the winch without binding. The stoppers will have to be bolted either through the deck or onto a sturdy platform because they will hold the full strain of the mainsail once the lines have been cranked in.

Such a system—roller headsail and cockpit reefing for the main—will be the simplest solution for most boats. With such a rig (and two reefs set up for the main) you will never have to leave the cockpit in winds up to 30 to 35 knots or so. Above that the main may have to come down, which will require a quick trip to the cabin top to tie in a few sail ties on the main that has been dropped into the lazy jacks.

But for those who want all controls led aft, you can set up a second battery of line stoppers on the other side of the companionway and add five or six more control lines to your cockpit repertoire. Further

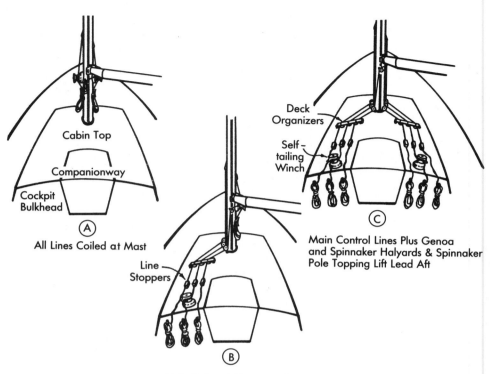

Three ways to arrange the halyards and lines running from the mast. (a) *This is the traditional way of keeping all lines at the mast. You always have to go forward and always to one spot to adjust lines.* (b) *Leading just the mainsail lines aft will mean you can avoid leaving the cockpit until it is time to put in a second reef or drop the main. This is good for coastal cruising, particularly if you have a roller headsail.* (c) *With all lines led aft, you can control the whole boat from the protection of the dodger.*

lines to bring aft should include: a third reefing line for the main sail; the headsail halyard; a second, spare headsail halyard; the main boom vang control, spinnaker halyard and the spinnaker boom topping lift. With all these lines terminating in the cockpit, a method will have to be devised to sort and stow them. On BOC boats, lines are stowed in canvas bags affixed to the inside of the cockpit and around the coaming. Once a halyard or line has been taken up, it can be coiled

*When setting up a system to lead lines aft, try to be logical about grouping lines together and strive to keep lines as low to the deck as possible. The fewer turns the lines have to make, the less the friction on them. Note that it will be impossible to stow gear on the cabin top without interfering with lines and halyards.*

*By using large-radius blocks, it is possible to have the halyards turn at the deck and remain very low to the deck. Also, note that using a double deck organizer will permit all lines to be led to one side, if you so desire.*

*Leading lines aft means there will always be a lot of loose tails to keep organized. Bags sewn of acrylic or netting can be used to catch loose lines and keep the cockpit tidy.*

and dropped into its bag. When it is time to let the line run free, remove it from the bag and uncoil it, removing possible knots, before flipping up the line stopper.

The rearranging of your halyards and lines aft to the cockpit will help a shorthanded crew enjoy sailing more in a wide range of conditions. If you rarely have to leave the protection of the cockpit dodger, then even sailing to windward in 30 knots and rain squalls won't be too bad. Well . . .

## ANCHORS AND RODES

Carrying the right anchors and ground tackle is a main concern for all sailors. No matter what conditions we meet out there in a far anchorage, we need to be able to hook the boat securely to the bottom, to protect it from grounding and protect ourselves from a suddenly wet visit to the beach. In Chapter Three we will discuss anchor types, rodes and windlasses in detail. Here we'll address the problem of stowing anchors on deck so that they are ready to be deployed but as out-of-the-way as possible.

Most coastal boats will carry only one anchor on deck that is attached to an anchor rode and ready to go over the side. The choice of which type you carry will depend upon the areas you sail, the bottoms you are trying to hook in to, and your own anchoring style. Yet the three anchors most commonly used are the lightweight Danforth-style, the plow and the Bruce. And all three are hard to stow on deck.

The best solution is to have your anchor nestled into a bow fitting tailored to its size and shape. Both plows and Bruce anchors can hang neatly on bow rollers, where they will be out of the way and ready to use. Bow rollers can be adapted to most boats and you will find a range of stainless-steel rollers available at larger chandleries and through mail-order houses. Remember that the strains on the anchor line will be transferred directly to the bow fitting. The stress can be particularly damaging when the boat is anchored in a choppy anchorage, causing the bow to pitch up and down. Make certain the roller is built of heavy steel and is solidly through-bolted and backed under the deck.

Stowing a Danforth-style anchor at the bow is more difficult. The simplest solution for coastal sailing is to hang the anchor from the bow pulpit in the patented straps available from most chandleries. Although not secure enough for sailing in rough conditions, this will keep the anchor at the ready and out of the way of those on the foredeck. Traditionally, Danforth-style anchors have been stowed in chalks on deck or on the cabin top. The chalks, which enable you to tie the anchor down neatly, are simply screwed to the deck, and the anchor is then tied in place with a short lanyard. If there is room enough on the foredeck to stow the anchor well forward, then such an installation will not be too inconvenient. If, however, you have to mount the anchor on the cabin top, you will find it a struggle each time you set the hook.

There are many ingenious ways boat owners have found to stow Danforth-style anchors, from lashings on the pulpit, to stainless-steel hawse pipes angled overboard, to customized brackets under a bowsprit. Each boat owner who wants to carry a Danforth-style will have to find the stowing method that works best for his or her boat.

Stern anchors are standard equipment on many ocean-sailing boats but are less common on coastal boats. For most of us a light lunch hook—smaller than our main anchors—will suffice. On *Clover* we stow our lunch hook–stern anchor in a cockpit locker, where it can be retrieved quickly and easily. Because I like to keep our decks as uncluttered as possible, we have chosen not to mount the anchor on the stern pulpit. Yet that is the best place for it if you have the space and can arrange the anchor rode in a compartment belowdecks. Center-cockpit boats and those with large aft decks can mount stern anchors on a roller for quick deployment. Most of us will have to find a way to lash the anchor to the pulpit or in chalks on deck. A small Danforth-style anchor may be the best choice here simply because you can hang it neatly on the stern rails in anchor hooks and then lash it tightly in place.

Storm anchors—a large fisherman, plow or even a large Danforth-style—should be stowed belowdecks or at the bottom of a sail locker. The object is to keep the weight of the anchor and its rode as low and as near the middle of the boat as possible. On *Clover* we keep our 75-pound Danforth-style storm anchor lashed to floors and brackets in the bilge next to the drive shaft. The 300 feet of nylon rode lives at the bottom of the forward sail locker. And 60 feet of ⅜-inch chain lives in an unused sump between the afterberths. If we were to carry a fisherman anchor, our choice would be the Luke version of the Herreshoff anchor, which can be disassembled and stowed in pieces in the bilge. Simple wood brackets can be fashioned and fixed in place to hold the pieces out of the way and securely in place. In many years of cruising the world we have never needed to use the storm anchor. Yet we would never sail without it.

Lastly, the working anchor rode needs to be kept ready to set, yet stowed out of the way. Most production boats have a chain locker forward that can be used for an all-chain rode or for a line-and-chain rode. In either case the rode will pass through a hawse pipe on deck. With all chain you need to flake the chain side to side as it comes in to ensure that it won't bind on itself and prevent it from running out smoothly. To make chain self-stowing as it comes in, a simple slide can be built into the chain locker that will allow the chain to slide evenly into a neat pile. The slide should be covered with tin or copper to protect the surface and to make it slippery. An all-line rode—with 6 to 20 feet of chain on the end—can be stowed in the chain locker also, although you will find that it will have to be hand-fed down through the deck hawse pipe. With nylon line you will find that it tends to kink under the deck as it is being paid out during anchoring. To avoid this as much as possible, make sure the hawse pipe is as large as you can have it. Additionally the line can be trained somewhat by towing it behind the boat and then coiling it wet and letting it dry in the sun. This will give the rope fibers firmness and help build a memory into the line. When the rode has hardened up a bit, with use and coiling, you will find that it will nearly coil itself belowdecks as you feed it down and will run freely when paid out.

## BIG ITEMS: LIFE RAFTS, WINDSURFERS, AWNINGS, ETC.

The longer you cruise and the longer you own your boat, the more you will have to contend with deck gear. What usually starts out as a sleek, uncluttered deck can become a jumble of items all lashed to the deck and the rig. If you cruise with children, the addition of big items to the deck is even more of a problem.

The big items we'll deal with here are: spinnaker poles, life rafts, sail boards and surfboards, scuba gear and awnings. Dinghies are their own special problem.

Even if you don't carry a spinnaker or a cruising chute, it is wise to carry a pole with which to wing out the genoa. Running dead downwind, there is no better rig for a sloop without a chute than wing-and-wing. A telescoping whisker pole of the type made popular by Forespar may be the best solution in this instance because it can be used effectively with genoas and jibs of different sizes. If you carry a cruising chute or a full spinnaker, you will carry a standard spinnaker

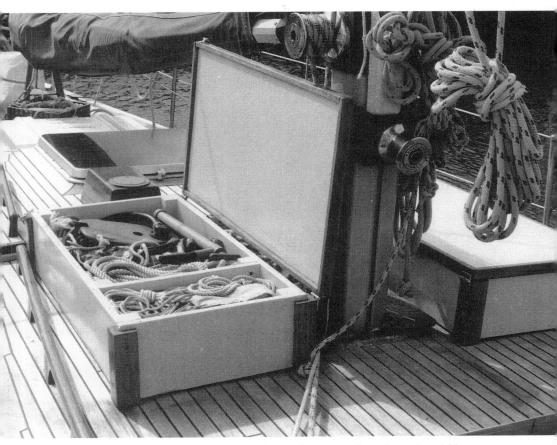

*Keeping the decks clear can be a struggle. Deck boxes such as these aboard* Clover *help us to fight the clutter while keeping useful gear handy.*

pole. Aboard *Clover* we carry both. The whisker pole is used for poling out the Yankee or small genoa, and the big pole is used for the spinnaker and the large genoa.

The simplest way to stow poles is in chalks fixed to the deck—one on either side of the foredeck. Forespar, Hall Spars and other rigging companies carry a wide range of cast aluminum or stainless-steel chalks for varying pole sizes. When these are installed on deck, be sure to space them so that the poles sit in them tightly to prevent the pole from rattling as the boat rolls or pitches. With the poles set up in this way, one person can manage the foredeck. The pole ends are freed from the chalks, the inboard end attached to the car on the mast and then the outboard end rigged with the guys and sheets needed. The whole pole itself need never he lifted at once, and all the heavy work can be handled by the topping lift and the foreguy.

Yet, a simpler solution is to rig the pole—or even both poles—on the mast. The mast track and cars will have to be able to slide virtually to the spreaders, and need to be rigged with both an uphaul for the cars and a downhaul. When deployed, the lower-outboard end of the pole is detached from the mast and the inboard end is lowered until the pole is in the correct position. Then the pole can be rigged with sheets and guys and hoisted into position with the topping lift. The beauties of such an arrangement are the simplicity of deploying the pole and the neatness of stowing the pole on the forward edge of the mast where no one will trip over it. Yet you should be aware that stowing a pole aloft adds weight where you don't want it. If your boat is already tender, you will only increase the tenderness by stowing the pole up the mast. However, most modern sloops carry enough beam and enough initial stability to make the addition of a few pounds aloft relatively meaningless.

Stowing a life raft is always a problem. You want it to be handy to the cockpit, if possible, yet as out-of-the-way and unobtrusive as possible. The two requirements do not go together easily. Probably the best place to stow a raft is under the helmsman's seat. However, the cockpit has to be designed and built with this in mind or space will not be available. On some modern designs, a life-raft compartment is built into the transom, where steps lead down from the cockpit. While this arrangement gets the raft out of the way, it also puts it in a place that would be impossible to get at in a large and breaking sea.

Most offshore sailors choose to mount the raft on the cabin top or on the foredeck. Both spots are out-of-the-way and can be reached in terrible sea conditions. If you choose to carry the raft on the foredeck, make certain that it is secured with straps that will withstand the force of breaking waves. Even in moderate conditions, when beating to windward in most boats you will find that from time to time a sea breaks right across the foredeck. A poorly secured raft could easily come adrift and you could find yourself with an inflated raft trailing

*Life rafts are big and can be difficult to stow on deck. The most common place is on top of the cabin. An acrylic cover will protect the raft and the fittings tying it to the deck.*

*Some rafts can be equipped with mounting frames. If so, these will require a lot of deck space. If the raft and frame are equipped with an hydrostatic release, the installation needs to be away from the rigging and mainsheet so that the raft can float free of the boat.*

astern. A hydrostatic release for the raft is an option you will want to study. Such release will free the raft from its deck seat should your boat sink under you before you can free the raft. A sound safety precaution, the hydrostatic release also increases the size of the raft and will make it harder to stow conveniently.

The life raft without a hydrostatic release should be seated on teak chalks and held in place with sturdy webbing. The webbing needs to have a quick-release buckle made of stainless steel or high-impact plastic. Providing a canvas cover will protect the raft and fastenings from sun damage.

More and more sailors are carrying sail boards and surfboards with them as they explore the coasts, and there may be nothing harder to stow effectively than a 11-foot 6-inch plastic board. When board sailing first became popular in the early 1980s, several manufacturers came out with brackets for carrying a board outside the lifelines. These are still the best solution for carrying a board on deck on smaller boats while coastal cruising. Yet it is also common to see boards simply tied inside the lifelines sitting on foam pads to protect the deck. The greatest danger in carrying a board tied to the lifelines is taking a wave across the foredeck and losing the board or tearing loose the stanchions. When going offshore the boards should be secured on the cabin top. Even better, if you have davits for the dinghy, the boards can be secured on the top of the davits where they will be well out-of-the-way of a breaking sea.

Sails, masts and booms all need to be tucked away somewhere on deck. The simplest way to stow the sails and masts is to remove the battens from the sails, roll them around the masts and then lash them to the sidestays. If you will be leaving the sails stowed this way for a long period, you should make tubelike sail covers to protect the sailcloth. Another approach is to use two-piece masts that can be disassembled and tucked into storage bags kept on the cabin top. A 10-foot bag tied down on the cabin top can hold the masts, booms, mast step fittings, center boards and even the rolled sails.

Scuba gear is heavy and delicate at the same time. The bottles need to be stowed in such a way that they cannot get loose in bad weather and cannot be damaged. Regulators, weight belts, flotation vests, wet suits, and so forth all need to be stowed so that they are dry, protected and out-of-the-way. The best place for scuba tanks is in the bottom of a deep cockpit locker, where they can be strapped into place. The rest of the gear should be kept in strong dive bags that can be tucked

*For large deck items such as sail boards, boogie boards, surfboards and more, a simple acrylic bag can be useful. Tied along the forward stanchions, this is Clover's "garage." Because it catches waves in rough head seas, the garage is mounted on the cabin top when sailing offshore.*

away in a lazarette or forward in a sail or chain locker. If the scuba gear is too hard to get at, you will find you use it less often than if it is readily accessible.

Those of us who spend a lot of time in warm climates and the tropics need to carry awnings that will provide shade over the cockpit and main decks. These can be big, bulky and hard to stow, for the best ones have solid cross members that will be as long as the width of the boat. If you intend to stow the awnings belowdecks, the cross-members need to be in two pieces. The awning then can be disassembled, folded, and stowed in a bag tailor-made for it. But it is simpler to leave the cross-pieces in one piece. The awning will be stronger, easier to put up and simpler to build. Such a contraption, which can be 15 feet long, can be stowed in a bag on the cabin top, or it can be lashed to the sidestays on the mainmast. Stowed in the shrouds, the awning will add a bit of windage and weight aloft, but it will be out-of-the-way and handy when you want to put it up.

## DINGHIES AND DAVITS

It is important for boats sailing offshore, even if only on short runs along the coast, to be able to carry the dinghy or dinghies securely on deck. If you carry a hard dinghy, you will find that there will be only a few ways to carry the dinghy. An inflatable is easier to carry and easier to hoist onto the deck, but you may not wish to deflate a dinghy each time you bring it aboard. Lastly, two-part dinghies, which have been developed to solve the deck-stowing problem, are a good solution, although the dinghies available commercially are very expensive.

In the past decade inflatable dinghies have taken over the sailing scene. This is because they are fast under outboard power, easy to mend, light and seaworthy. Aboard *Clover* an inflatable is our first choice, and a sailing dinghy a second choice—two dinghies being the ideal. Stowing an inflatable on deck requires only that there be enough space for it to lie upside down. You will find that deflating the dinghy is impractical for short runs, so you will generally leave it inflated and will have to find a spot for it on deck. This can either be on the cabin top or on the foredeck of an aft-cockpit sloop or on the afterdeck of a center-cockpit design. If space is at a premium, an inflatable can be partially deflated and wedged in almost anywhere. The best arrangement I've seen for stowing an inflatable on deck was aboard the 66-footer *Dione*, which Brian and Judy Harrison sailed around the world and now charter in the Caribbean. Their large—13-foot—inflatable, with its outboard still on the stern, can be hoisted on the mizzen boom right onto a small cradle on the afterdeck. Electric winches certainly take the sweat out of this job, but are not completely necessary. In three minutes the dinghy is on deck, tied down and *Dione* is ready to go.

Aboard *Clover* we carry the dinghy—8-foot 6-inch Avon, soft bottom with a rigid transom—on deck almost every time we go sailing simply because dragging it costs us half a knot or more. We stow it on the main cabin top, where it fits neatly aft of the mainmast and over the main saloon hatch. We bought this size, in fact, because it fit neatly on deck. To get it on deck, we hoist it with the main halyard and drop it on the side deck—it weighs only 85 pounds. Finally, with one person at the bow and another at the stern, we hoist it over the main saloon hatch and lash it to the cabin-top handrails. Including the time it takes to hoist the outboard onto its rack on the stern pulpit, lash the gas tank to the mainmast, stow oars, pump and sundries, and hoist the dinghy onto the deck, the whole job can be done by two of us in less than five minutes. However, a larger inflatable or a rigid dinghy would not be so easily handled.

Stowing a rigid or hard dinghy aboard requires some form of built-in solution. Most hard dinghies will not sit easily on deck without the aid of wood chalks for the bow and stern. These can be as elaborate as you like, or as simple. They need only be shaped to hold the bow in place and offer the stern a pad onto which it can be tied. Most often the best place to stow the hard dinghy is on the cabin top, yet larger boats will be able to find a spot forward of the mast if necessary. If you stow the dinghy upside down, it will present the lowest profile and offers a cave under which you can stow an inflatable or other gear. The chalks for such an arrangement can be small and unobtrusive. There are some who like stowing their dinghies upright on deck, requiring a large cradle for it to sit in. On boats of 50 feet or more this might be practical—as it was with the inflatable aboard *Dione*. Smaller boats will find such an arrangement wastes space and creates a monster on deck.

If you are determined to carry a hard dinghy and have it on deck, then a two-part dinghy may be the solution. Naval architect and cruising sailor Danny Greene has spent years perfecting two-part designs and offers several excellent sets of plans through the classified ads in the back of *Cruising World* magazine. These are plywood, stitch-and-tape dinghies that can be built for a few hundred dollars by any reasonably handy amateur. The beauty of the two-part dinghies is the light weight of the individual parts and the ease with which they can be hoisted on deck or launched. Finally, with a two-part boat, a 12-foot dinghy that rows and sails beautifully will stow on deck in a space under 8 feet long.

The one drawback to the two-part design is the difficulty of launching and assembling the dinghy in really bouncy conditions. If you have the dinghy stowed on deck and suddenly need to set a second anchor in choppy, windy weather, you'll find it nearly impossible to assemble the dinghy in the water. You'll have to put it together on deck and then manhandle it—120 pounds or so—over the side. In this situation an inflatable with an outboard is the best dinghy going.

The problem of how to store a dinghy out of the water while under

*On larger vessels it is possible to stow a hard dinghy in a small cradle on deck. The dinghy can become a catchall for loose deck gear. It is secure when stowed this way and can be launched and retrieved with the main halyard. However, in a big seaway, the dinghy is high and unprotected and could be lost to a breaking sea.*

*For coastal cruising, davits provide an excellent way to carry a hard dinghy. Most sailors stow hard dinghies on deck during passages.*

way can be solved most easily with davits. There are a dozen different davits available on the market, so there should be one model to suit your boat. Davits need to be mounted robustly so that they can carry a lot of weight canterlevered off the stern. Moreover, should you find yourself in rough weather with the dinghy still on the davits, the dinghy and the davits can create a lot of strain on the deck and davit fittings. A dinghy held in davits for a long period needs to be able to drain rainwater that would otherwise fill it, adding a huge amount of weight on the davits.

Davits usually have hoist cranks built into them and most often the gear ratio is small, making the job of raising a large dinghy hard work, particularly if the outboard has been left on the transom. You will find it easier to have two people cranking. Moreover, the gears are exposed to the weather and need to be cleaned and greased regularly. Once the dinghy is in place, it should be lashed tightly to the davits and the boat. In a seaway the swinging of a dinghy can put a hole in the dingy hull and can tear the davits from the deck. Chafe gear should be fitted where necessary.

When heading offshore, you should take the dinghy off the davits and mount it securely on deck. A large following sea could rip the dinghy loose and tear away the davits, creating a problem that could quickly endanger the dinghy and crew. In addition, when sailing in rough weather, you will want the weight of the dinghy inboard rather than hanging out over the stern, where it will increase the pitching motion of the boat and slow you down.

The last clumsy item to store related to the dinghy is an outboard. Most often you will find cruising boats with their outboards mounted on fitted boards on the stern pulpits. This is serviceable on most boats and in most weather conditions. But the engine is vulnerable here, and a larger engine—10 hp and up—will add weight and strain to the rail. When you anticipate sailing in rough waters or making a pass in high latitudes, bring the engine inboard, either down below or onto the cabin top, where it won't be swept by a breaking wave.

Other places to store an outboard on deck include at the sissy bars by the mainmast, down in a deep sail locker or in the shower stall of a large head. Wherever it is stowed for a passage, the engine must be tied down firmly to keep it from migrating about. It is heavy and sharp and could cause serious damage if it got loose.

## COCKPIT STRUTS AND ARCHES FOR RADAR, SOLAR PANELS AND ANTENNAE

For years power boat builders have installed arches and struts on larger power boats to carry radar domes and antennae. This idea was picked up by singlehanded racers in the OSTAR and BOC Challenge. From there struts and arches have begun to appear on many offshore cruising boats.

A single strut or pole is an excellent way to mount the radar and one or two antennse above head level on a sloop. Positioned well aft and braced against the stern pulpit, a single pole strut made of stainless-steel tubing is easy to install and will be strong and useful. The radome mounts stop the pole on a square of aluminum. The pole should be tall enough—8 feet or so—to keep the radar well above the crew

*The simplest way to mount electronics and antennae on a strut is atop a single pole positioned at the transom. The pole can carry a wide range of gear. It should be securely bolted and backed to the deck and made fast to the stern rail.*

level to avoid as much as possible the low-level radiation emitted from the unit. The base needs to be well braced, through-bolted on the deck and backed with a thick aluminum plate.

The simplest addition to the radar strut is antennae that do not require height—GPS and SatNav. The neatest way to add these is to have smooth tube elbows of about 1-inch diameter welded to the top sides of the strut—so the whole construction looks like a Sonora cactus. The antennae can then be attached to the tops of the elbows. It is possible in this way to add up to three antennae to the single-pole strut, with the third positioned aft. Be sure to check with the dealer or manufacturers of your GPS or SatNav to determine if the receiver will be damaged by radiation from the radar. The SatNav antenna, in particular, is alive, as it carries a low, 12-volt current.

Putting an arch across the boat will give the boat a new look—for better or worse—and will give you a number of options for mounting electronics and other gear. The simplest type of arch is fabricated of 1-inch stainless-steel tube, with welded cross-members on the top and through bolts at the deck. The frame must be strong enough to take the full weight of a large person thrown against it—500 pounds or more of force. A more complicated way to manufacture an arch is to mold up the shape from foam coring and fiberglass. While this is workable in production runs, a custom fiberglass arch will be too expensive for most owners.

When planning an arch, think through all the different jobs you want to do. An arch is a good platform for radar and antennae. You can mount all of your antennae above head level, but within easy reach of the cockpit for repairs. The only antenna that should not be installed here would be for the VHF, which needs to be as high as possible—VHF broadcasts only over a line-of-sight distance.

Yet the arch can also be a base for solar panels, which should be secured either horizontally or in pivoting frames. While this may seem to be adding a lot of weight and complexity at the stern and above an aft cockpit, panels mounted here can offer shade and protection as well as amps for your battery bank. The arch can act as the aft end of a cockpit awning which stretches aft from the aft end of a cockpit dodger. The easiest and possibly best installation is to have the awning rolled and stored under the arch. A fabric and Velcro closure will hold it neatly in place when not in use. When pulled out over the cockpit, the awning will slant slightly forward and can be pulled tight with webbing straps that lead to eye hooks forward of the dodger. In

*A cockpit arch of the type made popular by long-distance ocean racers permits the radar and other antennae to be mounted in a convenient spot. Moreover, if rigged with an awning, the arch can provide the after end of a cozy cockpit tent.*

addition, the arch can house a cockpit light for evenings in warm climates, or a fresh water hose for quick showers on the transom after swimming, or it can have a small stainless-steel arm-and-tackle incorporated into the design for lifting a heavy outboard engine from the dinghy to the stern pulpit. In my years of cruising, most recently in the cruising grounds of the South Pacific, I have seen arches used in many imaginative and useful ways. Once you decide you want one, all you have to do is dream up uses for it.

## Further Reading

*The Annapolis Book of Seamanship,* by John Rousmaniere (New York: Simon & Schuster, 1989).

*Offshore Cruising Encyclopedia,* by Steve and Linda Dashew (Ojai, Calif.: Beowulf Publishing Group, 1991).

*Safety at Sea,* by George Day (New York: G.P. Putnam's Sons, 1991).

*Spurr's Boat Book,* by Dan Spurr (Camden, Me.: International Marine Publishing, 1984).

# Chapter Three

# ANCHORING THE EASY WAY

*How to choose the right anchors and rodes for cruising.*

▲ Understanding Loads

▲ The Right Anchors

▲ Rodes for Cruising

▲ Windlasses

We had just got our primary anchor down and holding when the squall came through. It was a black beast of a thing that switched the wind 90 degrees and kicked up whitecaps all over the lagoon. *Clover* was anchored in the atoll of Manihi in the Tuamotu Archipelago of French Polynesia. We had put the anchor down in a corner of the lagoon protected from the trade winds. Now, the wind was due north and we had our stern hard on the coral ledge that fringed the beach. Behind us, in the surge, the yellow teeth of coral chewed the water and spat spray into the air.

There was no place to move to, so we quickly set out our second anchor and put a second snubber on the all-chain rode. For two hours, as the squall lashed us with 30-knot gusts and heavy rain, we ran the engine, stood an anchor watch, and kept our fingers crossed. *Clover's* bow rose and fell, sometimes violently, as we snubbed back on our ground tackle. Yet despite what might seem a precarious situation, we were never terribly concerned. We had faith in the anchors holding us. When it was over, we swung around to lie to the trades, and all was quiet again.

Others in the lagoon weren't so fortunate. One sloop snapped his snubbing line on the chain rode and pulled the windlass off the deck. Another let out so much chain that his anchor and rode became hopelessly tangled in coral heads. And a third, a boat left unattended, snapped her ground tackle and washed up onto the white sand beach at the island's eastern side. The boat was soon off again, but the hull was badly scratched and the keel gouged by coral.

It is situations like the one in Manihi—a sudden change in the weather requiring superior holding from your anchors—that should be the basis for deciding which anchors you will carry, how you will equip them with rodes and what anchor techniques you will have in your repertoire. Such situations were the model we based *Clover's* anchoring systems on. On the whole we have remained fairly secure on our hooks, although we have dragged a few times in areas with poor holding.

We subscribe to the principle that the working anchor should not be of the size recommended by authorities—this book or anyone else— but should be as large as you can comfortably handle. For our Mason 43 the normal recommended anchor is a 44-pound CQR, 44-pound Bruce or a 35-pound Danforth-style. This would be set on a 10-foot length of 5/16 chain and 250 feet of 1/2-inch nylon. That might suffice.

But we have a large and powerful Lofrans windlass on the bow, which makes it possible to use a different system. Our working anchor is 30-kilogram (66-pound) CQR on 250 feet of 3/8 chain. Our second anchor is a 44-pound Bruce on 20 feet of 3/8 chain and 250 feet of 3/4-inch nylon. Our storm anchor is a 75-pound Danforth-style with 100 feet of 3/8 chain and 300 feet of 1-inch nylon. With main and secondary anchors set, we have effectively two and a half times the holding power of normal working anchors. With the storm anchor set, the holding power goes up to four times the nominal level.

There are plenty of experienced sailors who will scoff at such an array of anchoring weapons, and they have a point. Anchors of the recommended size will do the job in almost all winds and in most anchoring conditions. Moreover carrying around the weight at the

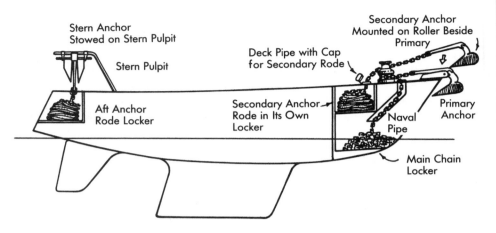

*Setting up a versatile anchoring system will require the ability to deploy three anchors quickly: a primary hook, a second anchor at the bow and a stern anchor. Having the rodes stowed neatly in their own lockers, with anchors on their own rollers, will make using the gear easier.*

bow that *Clover* does increases the boat's pitching motion in a choppy sea. It's a compromise, and we've opted for more rather than less.

Whichever way you intend to go with anchors and rodes, it is wise to start with an understanding of loading on the gear.

## UNDERSTANDING LOADS

When you set out to choose anchors for your boat, you should have in mind the amount of strain that anchor—and its rode and deck hardware—will have to sustain to hold you firmly. The primary strain on your anchor tackle will be the force exerted on the boat by the force of the wind. This exerts what amounts to a straight-line force, and the accompanying table gives a general guide to the loading on various hull lengths and beams in varying wind strengths. When reading the figures, remember that split-rigged boats—yawls, ketches and schooners—or those with baggy wrinkle, lazy jacks, a crow's nest aloft and so forth will present more windage and thus will exert a larger force on the ground tackle. Conversely, fractionally rigged sloops with little rigging and nothing aloft may exert slightly less windage and less force on the tackle.

*Clover*, a 43-foot, 12-foot-beam ketch with lazy jacks, will exert approximately 20 percent more windage than a comparable sloop. Therefore to figure the loads she will create in 42 knots of wind, I take the 40-foot base of 2,400 pounds and add 10 percent for the extra 3 feet of length and extra beam to arrive at 2,640 pounds. Then I add a further 20 percent for the additional windage and arrive at an approximate force figure of 3,012 pounds in 42 knots of wind. In 60 knots the force is approximately 6,436 pounds.

Once you have an idea of the amount of force your boat will exert on the ground tackle, there are two types of loads you should consider that will affect your anchors and tackle: tensile strength and shock loads. Tensile strength is the inherent strength of the metal anchor and chain when subjected to a constant load. The measure of such a strength will give you an idea of how strong an anchor is, particularly in comparison to other similar anchors. This is useful information. But it is not the whole story. In use, anchors are also subject to sudden loads—shocks—when caught under coral or ledge in a rough anchorage. The force exerted by the bow of a 15-ton cruising boat lurching back on its rode with full force will be enormous, possibly two or three times the loads exerted while the hull is not pitching. There has been some excellent test work done on tensile strength in

| Boat Dimensions* | | Horizontal Loads in Pounds | | | |
|---|---|---|---|---|---|
| LOA | Beam | Wind 15 knots | Wind 30 knots | Wind 42 knots | Wind 60 knots |
| 20' | 7' | 90 | 360 | 720 | 1,440 |
| 30' | 9' | 175 | 700 | 1,400 | 2,800 |
| 40' | 12' | 300 | 1,200 | 2,400 | 4,800 |
| 50' | 15' | 400 | 1,600 | 3,200 | 6,400 |
| 60' | 17' | 500 | 2,000 | 4,000 | 8,000 |
| 70' | 20' | 675 | 2,700 | 5,400 | 10,800 |
| 80' | 22' | 900 | 3,600 | 7,200 | 14,400 |

*Use LOA or beam of your boat, whichever produces the largest load value.

*The force of wind against your boat will be the basic determining factor of what type and size of anchors you choose. The figures above are only estimates. To arrive at a safe working load for your boat, you will have to increase the figure for extra windage or decrease it if the boat has a low profile and low windage. (The chart was adapted and revised by the author from material that originally appeared in* Cruising World *magazine.)*

anchors and rodes. But as far as I know, no work has been done to simulate real-life shock loads, so your estimates are as good as mine.

The best research done on tensile strengths was undertaken by the Boating Safety Division of Boat/US and *Cruising World* magazine. The results of the tests were published in a report by then executive editor Betsy Gooding in the May 1989 issue of *Cruising World,* along with the results of anchor-manufacturer-sponsored anchoring tests run by Rule Industries and by Simpson-Lawrence.

The object of the tensile-strength test was to gain a benchmark for assessing how much strain an anchor hooked on coral or rock can withstand before it fails. The tests run by *Cruising World* and Boat/US were not intended to measure holding power but ultimate strength. In other words, while an anchor might exhibit a holding power of 5,000 pounds when buried in mud, how would it do when wedged by the tip into an immovable obstruction? It is a very pertinent test, for no matter how careful we are to avoid rocks and coral when we set our anchors, in many parts of the world the likelihood of encountering rocks or coral is quite high.

The tensile tests were conducted by Com-Tex Development Corp. in Lowell, Massachusetts. To simulate actual strain while in use, the tips of the anchors or the flukes were hooked in a strop while a measurable force was applied. Six anchors were tested, in two general groups: burying fluke anchors of the lightweight or Danforth-style and hooking anchoring of the CQR- and Bruce-style.

The results were not too surprising. The light, fluke anchors—Danforth-style—which depend upon the surface area of their flukes and burying ability for holding strength, did not show a high tensile strength when "hooked." The indication is, then, that should you get your Danforth-style anchor caught on a piece of coral or a ledge with one of its flukes, you might well bend the anchor. Additionally the stocks and crown plates of the Danforth-style anchors tend to break under extreme loads.

The second group included CQR-types and Bruce anchors, which depend upon hooking and burying for their holding power. These, as might be suspected, were considerably more durable in the tensile-strength tests. The CQR, which is made of drop-forged steel, and the Bruce, which is made of heat-treated cast steel, held their shapes at two and three times the force of the fluke-type anchor. The Danforth plow-type, which is called a Deepset anchor, is welded and failed at less than half the force of the CQR.

The indication from the test results is that in situations in which hooking onto something hard is liable to be your method of anchoring, then a cast or forged-steel anchor of the hooking type should be your choice. Moreover if you know you will be anchoring in a wide range of anchorages, all with different or uncertain bottoms, then a hooking anchor that also buries reasonably well may well be the best compromise.

Loading does not only affect the anchor, but it also affects the chain and any rope rode you have in your ground tackle. If you choose an anchor that can withstand 10,000 pounds of load and attach it to your boat with chain that only rates at a breaking strength of 4,000 pounds, you have thrown away most of your anchor's potential. As you go through the process of deciding what anchors to carry and the rodes to attach them to the boat, keep in mind that the tested breaking strengths of chain and nylon line are maximum limits of the force to be applied to them. And keep in mind as well that in conditions that might put more force on your tackle than it is rated for, you should have a second anchor ready to take up the extra load.

# THE RIGHT ANCHORS

As we have discussed above, choosing the right anchors for your boat is an exercise in determining the forces involved, the strengths of the anchors and tackle, and your anchoring style—in other words whether you like to anchor with one or two anchors. Yet the first thing to remember when selecting anchors is that as you cruise the coasts, you will find many different bottoms into which you want to hook your anchor. You will find hard sand and soft sand, mud and ooze, clay and shale, coral sand and marl, rocks and kelp and coral heads. If you are going to be cruising, then you should carry an anchor or two or more anchors that can cope with all these different conditions. There has been a lot of discussion about which anchors hold best and a lot of media hype created by anchor manufacturers. There have been public tests and there have been detailed published test results. Yet all of the tests are, to my mind, suspect because they have been run by the manufacturers for public-relations reasons. You will never see an anchor doing poorly in a test run by its manufacturers, although the test run by his competitor showed the anchors in question to be useless.

*Two working anchors on a heavy stainless-steel roller will provide the holding power you need in almost all circumstances. This type of arrangement is popular in the offshore cruising fleet. For coastal cruising in calm weather one anchor will almost always be sufficient.*

When selecting a main anchor, it only makes sense to choose one that will serve you well on the widest variety of bottoms. That's not to say you shouldn't specialize if you know you will always encounter a special anchoring situation. For example, if you know you will be anchoring in river mud every time you go out, you should choose a burying anchor with wide flukes—such as a Danforth-style or the new Fortress anchors. If you know you will normally be anchoring in rocks and kelp, then you need a hooking anchor that can penetrate layers of seaweed and then grab onto a ledge—a Herreshoff, a fisherman's or yachtsman's anchor. But most of the time you will be anchoring in sand and rock or mud and rock, as these are the two most common items at the bottoms of bays, estuaries and harbors. For this range of bottoms a general-purpose anchor is the best choice.

Also, when selecting an anchor it is important to remember what an anchor really does for you under the water: It must be easy to set in the conditions under you; it must be able to provide holding power sufficient to keep the boat from dragging; and it must be able to reset itself without fouling on the anchor rode when the wind or current changes. This last point is critical. The wind and/or the current always change. In light conditions you can count on it. In moderate conditions it happens often, when the sea breeze becomes the night breeze or the prevailing wind shifts after sunset. In storm conditions a shift can be predicted and should be known in advance so that a second anchor can be deployed in the right direction if need be. Your anchor needs to be able to break free, turn itself over and reset itself smartly. Not all specialty anchors will do this. A fisherman's anchor, for example, will reliably foul itself on the fluke when the wind changes; and a Danforth-style will be caked with mud or clay when it breaks free and may take some time to reset.

It is hard to find an anchor that does not have at least a few vices. But seek out a primary anchor that fits your needs and can be used in a range of bottoms. If necessary a secondary and a storm anchor can be selected with specific bottoms in mind.

*Plow-type:* The plow is a venerable anchor type, with the CQR manufactured in Scotland by Simpson-Lawrence being the most widely known worldwide. However, every yachting nation has its own version of the anchor type, and many, but certainly not all, are as good as the original. A hooking anchor with plow-shaped flukes for holding in soft sand and mud, the plow may be the most versatile of popular anchors. Weight and angle of attack are critical in the successful use of the anchor. It will not like being set on scope of less that 5-to-1 of all chain or 7-to-1 of a nylon rode with a chain leader. The more scope, the better. Also, the anchor relies on weight to penetrate the bottom. The heavier it is, the more firmly it will set. Although difficult to store aboard, except on a bow roller, the plow is used as the primary anchor by most offshore and round-the-world cruisers.

*Bruce:* Originally developed to anchor drilling platforms in the North Sea, the Bruce is a one-piece cast-steel anchor that is both incredibly strong and quite versatile. With its three-pronged hooking design, there's no question that the anchor will grab coral and ledge better than any other type. However, because of its wide shape, it also buries itself in the sand or mud and will hold very well. Its design makes it easy to set, and it will hold at its maximum loading on quite short scope, 4-to-1 or even 3-to-1. Because it sets easily and quickly, it also resets well when the wind or current changes. Despite some test data offered by other anchor manufacturers, the Bruce has proven itself to be a superb anchor. Its main drawback is the difficulty of stowing it below or on deck. A bow roller is the only permanent solution.

*Delta:* A new anchor on the scene, the Delta is a hybrid of the best of the CQR design and the Bruce. A one-piece steel casting, it is a hooking anchor in many ways similar to the Bruce. Yet it has a point for penetrating hard sand bottoms and kelp that give it more versatility

*The Bruce anchor has gained wide popularity in the past few years. But it is difficult to stow, either on deck or on a bow roller. Here Jeanneau has come up with a unique roller system that works very well.*

than its three-pronged cousin. Like the CQR, it has flukes for holding in soft sand and mud. But the Delta's flukes are more obliquely angled and therefore present a broader, flatter surface than does the CQR—providing greater potential holding for the same size and weight. Like the two more famous anchors, the Delta is rapidly developing a following among experienced cruisers.

*Fortress:* A relatively new lightweight or Danforth-style anchor, the Fortress has made its name as a well-crafted and reliable burying anchor. It is notable for its incredibly high weight-to-holding ratios. Yet even though the manufacturer makes such claims, it seems unwise to choose the lightest possible anchor for your boat—unless you are equipping a racing boat. The newer models have adjustable flukes enabling you to either set it for sand and shell bottoms or for soft mud bottoms. In the latter conditions—ooze and swamp mud—the Fortress may have no equal.

*Standard lightweight or Danforth-type:* There are many anchors in this general category, including the Fortress mentioned above. The Danforth Company, part of Rule Industries, manufactures most of the lightweight, fluke anchors on the market in North America. These are either the standard fluke anchors of welded galvanized steel or the newer high-tensile models of higher grades of steel. There are a number of imitations on the market that are basically the same design as the Danforth but cost a third of the price. It makes sense to beware of the cheap imports, for they will not be built to the same quality as those with a brand name to protect. The fluke-type anchor gains its strength from its ability to bury itself quickly in soft sand and mud. The buried flukes then present a broad, flat surface, which prevents the anchor from dragging. Theoretically in deep, soft mud the anchor will continue to bury itself until it is many feet below the bottom level.

Once, when anchored aboard a 38-footer in a sandy-bottom harbor in southern Massachusetts, I weathered a 60-knot tropical storm. The boat weighed approximately 10 tons, and we were hanging on a 35-pound Danforth anchor with 8 feet of chain and 150 feet of ⅝-inch nylon. The tackle held admirably. And when it was time to get the hook up again, we had to raise it from a deep, muddy berth far below the eelgrass and sand.

*Fisherman's (yachtman's or Herreshoff) anchor:* This venerable design has been used by sailors for hundreds of years and was perfected in England in the eighteenth century. Until the advent of the plow and the Danforth-type, early in this century, the fisherman's anchor was the only choice for yachtsmen and commercial sailors alike. Today few cruising sailors carry the fisherman-type, because it is unwieldy, prone to fouling when the wind or current changes, and difficult to stow at the bow and down below. Yet as a hooking anchor with the ability to penetrate weed and kelp, the anchor is useful in some regions of the country—northern New England and the Pacific Northwest, in particular. Also, there are some offshore sailors who believe that a fisherman's anchor of great weight is the best storm anchor. In rocky and kelp-strewn waters I suspect they are right. The best anchor of this type is manufactured by Paul Luke and Co. of East Boothbay, Maine. The Luke anchor can be broken down into manageable parts,

*If you cruise in a wide range of areas, it makes sense to have two different types of anchors to get the best result. The plow on the right will work well in most conditions. But the Danforth-style on the left will do the best job in soft sand and mud.*

| Minimum Breaking Strengths for Ground Tackle (in Pounds) | | | |
|:---:|:---:|:---:|:---:|
| **Diameter** | **Three-strand** | | **Chain** |
| **(in inches)** | **Nylon Rope** | **BBB** | **High-Test** |
| ¼ | 1,800 | 2,600 | 6,500 |
| ⁵⁄₁₆ | 2,800 | 3,900 | — |
| ⅜ | 4,000 | 5,500 | 13,000 |
| ½ | 7,100 | 9,500 | 22,000 |
| ⅝ | 10,500 | 14,500 | 33,000 |
| ¾ | 14,200 | 20,500 | 46,000 |
| ⅞ | 19,000 | 24,000 | — |
| 1 | 24,600 | 31,000 | — |

*The breaking strengths of ground tackle should be considered the maximum loading acceptable for your boat. Selecting the right rode for the job involves a careful estimate of normal and maximum loads. You should then add in a margin of safety. (This chart was adapted by the author from a chart that originally appeared in* Cruising World *magazine.)*

which makes it easier to handle and easier to stow away below the boat's floorboards when not in use.

*Northill:* A specialty anchor, the Northill is constructed of welded stainless steel. It is a hooking-type anchor that derives its basic design from the fisherman's anchor. Like the fisherman's, it is prone to fouling when the wind or current change. But unlike the fisherman's anchor, the Northill is lighter and can be folded for storage. Not often used by offshore cruisers, the Northill will appeal to those who are attempting to save weight aboard.

## RODES FOR CRUISING

Unlike the choice of anchors, there are only a few ways to set up your rodes and tackle that have been widely accepted by cruising sailors. There are three things you want from your rodes: to be able to deploy and retrieve them easily; to have them strong enough to hold the boat in the highest winds you will be likely to meet; and to be durable enough to avoid chafing through no matter what bottom they lie upon.

For ease of handling, high strength for low weight and durability in most conditions, three-strand nylon line has no rivals. In addition, nylon's elasticity enables a boat to surge back on its ground tackle in bad conditions without exerting a jarring strain on the anchor below—a strain that could easily cause the anchor to break free and drag. Finally, nylon is inexpensive, providing a terrific amount of strength and peace of mind for the cost.

At the end of your nylon rode you will most likely want a length of chain that will do several things for you. The chain will give the rode catenary bend—the sag that holds the stock of the anchor in a downward position so that it can remain properly set in the bottom. Without a length of chain the rode will pull directly from the stock and will have a tendency to lift it and break the anchor free of the bottom. Yet the length of chain performs a second and equally vital role. Being immune to chafe, it protects your rode from parting due to contact with sharp objects on the bottom—rocks, coral or debris. It is common to use a 6- to 8-foot length of chain on your rode, particularly when using lightweight anchors such as the Danforth-style or Northill. Yet unless you are anchoring in pure sand or mud, you should be prepared to have the rode sweeping across rough and sharp objects on the bottom. For this reason it makes sense to have a longer length of chain—long enough to allow the end of the chain to swing free of the bottom. In addition, when using anchors that depend in part on their weight for their burying power—plow, Bruce, fisherman's—then the extra chain gives you an added measure of heft down where it counts. Aboard Clover we have rigged our second anchor—a 44-pound Bruce—with 20 feet of ⅜ chain. When anchored at 7-to-1 in 20 feet of water, with 140 feet of scope, we have observed that the end of the chain lifts free of the bottom when the rode straightens out, thereby allowing only chain to chafe on the bottom. This extra length of chain makes the anchor heavier to raise from the bottom, yet the protection and increased holding power more than compensate for the inconvenience. Also, an electric or hydraulic windlass will make the job a lot easier.

One note about nylon: Three-strand rope tends to pick up fine sand when it lies on the bottom. In areas of coral sand, which is very fine and quite abrasive, the line can become caked with sand. The sand inside the line chafes each strand and can destroy an otherwise sound rode when under strain for a few days. After anchoring in fine coral sand, trail your anchor rode astern for a while as you sail on to the next anchorage. This will remove most of the sand and will take out any kinks that may have appeared in the rope.

Sailors setting off for far anchorages or to regions of coral and rocky

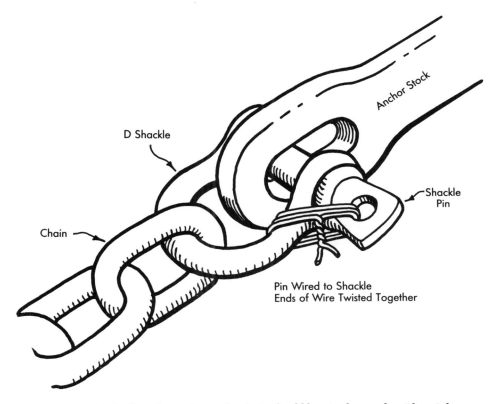

Anchor Stock

D Shackle

Shackle Pin

Chain

Pin Wired to Shackle
Ends of Wire Twisted Together

*The shackle holding the anchor to the chain should be wired securely with stainless steel or Monel Metal wire. The wire deteriorates in time and must be checked and renewed.*

bottoms will need to equip themselves with an all-chain rode. In the offshore cruising fleet chain is used without exception for the simple reason that nylon will not hold up to the abuse of anchoring daily in a wide range of different bottom conditions. There are several different types of anchor chain available—proof coil, high-test, stud-link, long-link and BBB—but only high-test and BBB are commonly used.

BBB is the chain you will see most often aboard offshore cruising boats. It costs less than high-test and offers a high strength for its weight. When in active use, BBB chain will last many years and can be regalvanized several times before the links finally wear down. With galvanized chain it is important to keep it clean of mud and to wash it before stowing it in the chain locker. Mud in the links will hold moisture that will cause the chain to rust prematurely, and once rusty, the chain links will chafe on each other, shortening the chain's life.

High-test chain is lighter and stronger for its weight and correspondingly more expensive. It should be treated with the same care as BBB chain and will offer many years of useful service. High test is the choice of those who want the very best on their anchor rode and of those who seek to save weight by using a smaller chain size. A third advantage of high-test chain is that you can carry a longer section for the same weight as a shorter length of BBB. Aboard *Clover* we carry 250 feet of BBB chain on our main anchor, which is only just enough. In French Polynesia we often had to anchor in 60 to 90 feet of water, which meant we could only use a 3-to-1 ratio. Were we to carry high-test, we would be able to use $\frac{5}{16}$ chain (twice the breaking strength of our $\frac{3}{8}$-inch chain) and could load an extra 100 feet into the chain locker without adding weight.

The problem with chain is its lack of stretch. In a choppy anchorage and in high winds the chain will tend to straighten out, putting a lot of strain on your deck gear and on the anchor. A galvanized chain hook and a length of nylon line well protected from chafe with a plastic hose or other chafe gear should be part of your anchor repertoire. In normal conditions only 4 feet or so of nylon should be let out, with an extra 3 feet of chain hanging loose. When the boat swings and takes up on the chain, the nylon will stretch and the chain will not snub up on itself. During the night, if you hear the chain working in the bow roller or if you hear it snub with a bang on the windlass, you'll know it's time to let out more nylon. We use a 50-foot length of $\frac{5}{8}$-inch line, as the snubber and have let out most of it on several occasions when the wind piped up over 30 knots. Also, we carry

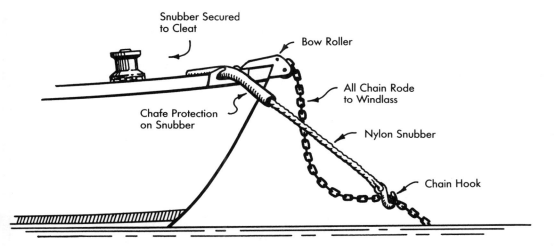

Snubber Secured
to Cleat

Bow Roller

Chafe Protection
on Snubber

All Chain Rode
to Windlass

Nylon Snubber

Chain Hook

*A three-strand chain snubber will protect your windlass from sudden shocks and will help prevent the anchor from jerking out of the bottom when the rode straightens out. The snubber should have a chain hook at one end and chafing gear where the line passes over the bow.*

a second chain hook in one of our deck boxes so that we can rig a second snubber if the first looks overloaded. We've only rigged the second snubber once, during a gale in Tonga that saw us anchored on a lee shore in a 2-foot chop. The big anchor held, the chain didn't chafe through on the coral heads on the bottom and the snubbers kept the chain from straightening out and breaking something.

Selecting your battery of anchors and rodes will depend upon where you intend to sail and anchor, the type of boat you own and your own anchoring style. Yet despite all the choices, it is prudent to use robust tackle, with heavy shackles (wired closed) and plenty of scope. You'll always sleep better and will enjoy even poor weather if you do.

# WINDLASSES

There are many laborsaving devices available to make life better afloat. But none, in my estimation, carries its own weight as consistently and as effortlessly as a good anchor windlass. In fact the windlass is the heart of your anchoring system.

If you sail without a windlass—few offshore cruisers do—then your anchors and rodes and the depths in which you anchor will all be limited to a weight one person can hoist. If you sail as a couple, then the weight should be no more than the smaller person can manage. In our case, Rosa weighs 115 pounds and could manage to get a 35-pound Danforth-style anchor with 6 feet of chain and 100 feet of rode on board if I were incapacitated. But she wouldn't do it more than once, unless she had to. And such a rig would be far too light for *Clover* in most conditions and most bottoms. Without a windlass we simply couldn't cruise as far and wide and as comfortably as we do.

The windlass you choose for your boat should be able to handle the most extreme conditions you may find. It must be able to hoist all of your chain and your heaviest anchor when hanging straight into deep water. Or it must be able to hoist your normal length of chain and your largest anchor even with a big piece of coral wedged into it. Or you should be able to kedge your boat off a sand bank.

There are three types of windlasses to choose from: manual, electric and hydraulic. Manual windlasses are the simplest to install, easiest to service and least complicated. The most common small manual windlass in the cruising fleet is the Simpson-Lawrence Sea Wolf. A double-action windlass, this unit will be a real aid on smaller boats.

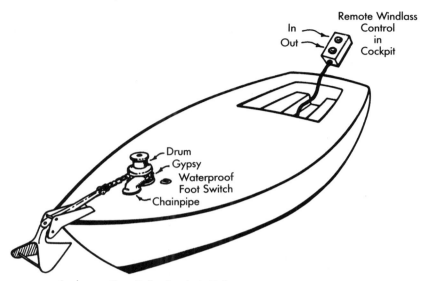

Anchor on Bow Roller Ready to Fall

*Living with a powerful windlass will make cruising easier and safer. If you are sailing shorthanded, it is possible to wire a remote control for the windlass to the cockpit so that the anchor can be operated from the helm.*

On larger boats the double-handle Goiot windlass, which is worked like a small coffee grinder, is an excellent unit, despite the use of dissimilar metals in the construction and hence the tendency to corrode.

Most boats in the 30- to 50-feet range can really benefit from en electric or hydraulic windlass. Not only will the windlass allow you to use heavier ground tackle, but it will mean you won't hesitate to change your anchorage—haul up all your gear—if the wind changes or you don't like how you're swinging. If you have to crank up the anchor and know it will take fifteen minutes of hard work, you're more likely to put off a move that could make the difference between a peaceful night and a sleepless one.

A wide range of electric windlasses are available from companies such as Lewmar, Lofrans, Maxwell, Nilsson and Ideal. And most companies build both vertical-axis and horizontal-axis units. Vertical-axis machines have the benefit of keeping all the electrical connections and the electric motor itself belowdecks, where it won't be subject to salt spray, sunlight and other abuse. Also, a vertical-axis windlass presents a lower profile and is less apt to become tangled in genoa sheets and mooring lines than a horizontal-axis device. Lastly, with a top-of-the-line vertical-axis unit—Lewmar, Maxwell, Nilsson and Lofrans—you will be able to fit a hawse pipe that will make your all-chain rode self-stowing belowdecks. The turn around the gypsy will be a full 180 degrees, which gives you the best grip on the chain and the most security.

Yet a horizontal-axis windlass, which is mounted on the foredeck with its motor and electrical connections exposed, has several qualities that make it excellent for offshore cruising. First, the electric motor is easier to reach and therefore easier to service than on a through-the-deck unit. Although most windlasses are relatively trouble-free, it is necessary to check and replace brushes on the motor from time to time, to check and top up gear oil and to keep the moving parts greased. If you can work on the windlass on the foredeck, then you're more likely to keep it in running order.

The second advantage to horizontal windlasses is relatively insignificant. When handling a nylon rode, the lead angle from the horizontal wildcat side of the unit will be comfortable and natural. From a vertical-axis unit you will find that you have to bend over to get a fair lead into a position that will be awkward.

Electrical windlasses require power, lots of it. A 100-pound pull from a moderate windlass—suitable for a 35-footer—will require up to 110 amps for approximately five minutes under high load, or approximately 20 amp/hours. If you use a large windlass and subject it to heavy use—400 pounds of pull for five minutes—you will have to crank out approximately 40 amp/hours to keep it going. That is a lot of draw on your batteries and will require either a large reserve battery capacity or a running generator or engine alternator.

On *Clover*, which has a reserve capacity of 400 amp/hours in her battery bank, we use a Lofrans horizontal windlass that was sold in Europe under the Atlas model name. It has a pull of approximately 500 pounds and requires, in average use, a draw of 90 to 120 amps during use. At maximum pull it uses over 250 amps or 50 amp/hours. To keep the batteries charged and happy, we always run our engine and high-capacity alternator while using the windlass. That way we can use the 400 reserve amps and the 110 amps of charging to maintain equilibrium.

Hydraulic windlasses have been around for years aboard fishing boats and commercial vessels already rigged with hydraulic systems. However, the engineering for an hydraulic windlass aboard a cruising boat is both sophisticated and expensive, so the technology has not been used widely. That said, Lewmar and Maxwell both offer excellent systems that are powerful and well designed for the marine environment. If you are installing hydraulics for the rig—backstay adjuster, boom vang and possibly powered winches—then an hydraulic windlass on the foredeck makes sense.

Whichever way you choose to go, a windlass will change the way you feel about anchoring and will allow you to explore deeper coves and set better anchors. You should sleep better and enjoy your time on the water more. If technology can do anything for sailing, it should help you accomplish that.

### Further Reading

*Anchoring,* by Brian Fagan (Camden, Me.: International Marine Publishing, 1986).

*Anchoring: All Techniques for All Bottoms,* by Don Bamford (Blue Ridge Summit, N.J.: Tab Books, 1987).

*The Complete Book of Anchoring & Mooring,* by Earl R. Hinz (Centerville, Md.: Cornell Maritime Press, 1986).

# Chapter Four

# THE SILENT CREW

*Overcoming the tyranny of the tiller.*

- ▲ Wind Vanes for Boats Under 50 Feet
- ▲ Wind Vanes for Larger Boats
- ▲ Autopilots

We were on our way from the tiny atoll of Mopelia in western French Polynesia to the kingdom of Tonga some 1,100 miles away. It was supposed to be a classic Pacific trade-wind crossing, but the trade winds had vanished and in their place we had turbulent swirling conditions with strong southerly winds and big running swells. Normally when the weather turns against us, we just cope, hunker down and let the self-steering carry us through. But on that trip disaster struck.

On the second night out, a night without stars or moon, we were charging along at 7 knots with two reefs in the main and half the Genoa rolled in and poled on the spinnaker pole. Suddenly *Clover* slewed off a wave and jibed all standing. The preventer on the main kept the boom from crossing the boat, but we were backwinded. We threw off the Sailomat self-steering, grabbed the wheel and jibed again, setting *Clover* back on her course. Then, with the confidence built over many thousands of miles of ocean sailing, I reached back and reset the wind vane so that it could continue to pilot us throughout the night. But it wouldn't engage. After a few minutes of fiddling with it I finally shone the flashlight over the stern to see what the problem might be. It was painfully obvious. The steering rudder on the Sailomat was gone. The rudder shaft had broken below the breakaway tube. And sadly the preventer line had slipped off. We carried two spare sacrificial tubes, which are designed to break in place of the rudder post. But we did not carry a spare rudder.

We stared at each other and at the wheel, which was then in Ross's hand. *Clover* does many things well. But sailing herself downwind or broad reaching in a big sea isn't one of them. We had 800 miles to go and we knew we would have to hand-steer all the way. We knew it would be hard work in the running seas, too hard for a three-hour watch, too hard for the boys to be able to help. It took five and a half days—two hours on and two hours off, twelve watches each a day, sixty-six watches in all.

At the end we sailed into Vavau with one thought in our minds: never again. Soon we had purchased a new autopilot from our friends Eric and Clara Urbahn, who had a spare aboard their magnificent boat, *Finback.* And, in Fiji—only a short hop away—we built a new rudder. We now cruise with a wind vane and autopilot and carry spares for both. Looking back, it amuses us to think that we had such faith in the Sailomat that we had elected not to install an autopilot earlier. In fact the old model 3040 Sailomat—no longer manufactured—is one of the best wind vanes ever built. By the time it failed, it had steered more than 40,000 sea miles over twelve years. Not bad at all.

Yet we are much taken with the new electric autopilot and use it all the time. It is a simple Autohelm 3000, cockpit mounted and linked to the main wheel with a rubber belt. Although designed for smaller boats, the 3000 handles *Clover* nicely in most conditions with only a nominal drain on the batteries. Were we to consider an autopilot our primary steering aid, we would install a more powerful unit— something like the Autohelm 6000 or the Robertson. As it is, our Sailomat continues to do the yeoman's duty, and the Autohelm fills in as necessary.

Our first principle when it comes to steering is: We don't, unless we have to. The second is that we will slow the boat if necessary to balance the helm to neutral (no weather or lee helm) in order to make either the vane or the autopilot's job easier. And, on longer passages, we will alter course to permit either device to steer comfortably, feeling confident that over time the wind will shift.

There are many other ways of rigging self-steering, many wind-vane units and many autopilots. Among the gear and the technology, there is a system that will be right for your boat.

## WIND VANES FOR BOATS UNDER 50 FEET

Wind vanes are marvelous devices and indispensable aboard offshore cruising boats. The two great advantages of wind vanes are their ability to keep a boat on a relative bearing to the wind and their pure energy efficiency. The first enables you to sail efficiently without fearing a wind shift—particularly a sudden flying jibe—while the second means you never have to feed your mechanical helmsman (sandwiches or electricity).

It is only just over thirty years ago that Blondie Hasler devised the first practical wind-driven steering unit. He used design concepts developed for model boats sailed in London's Hyde Park pond and adapted them to his oceangoing *Folkboat Jester.* The rig was operated by a large sail aft, which was trimmed to guide lines on the tiller. Used in the first Singlehanded Transatlantic Race in 1960 by Hasler and Francis Chichester, the device enabled the sailors to sail solo as efficiently as if they had crew. That race, which Chichester won aboard *Gypsy Moth,* really began the modern era of offshore cruising by demonstrating that small crews—particularly couples—could go to sea without the burden of steering or constantly trimming sails.

I vividly recall sailing my own small Beetlecat sailboat next to the moored *Gypsy Moth* that summer after Chichester had won the inaugural race. It was a large (to me) ocean-sailing vessel. It looked rugged and strong and wise in the ways of the sea. And the contraption on the stern was a marvel to behold. Its sail was very nearly as large as the gaff sail that propelled my little boat. And to a boy of ten it looked purposeful, exotic and as arcane as celestial navigation.

The design of self-steering units evolved quickly after that. Hasler's device grew a smaller sail and sprouted a servo-blade, which trailed in the water and, when activated by the sail to catch the force of water flowing by the boat, gave the device much more power. From this basic idea came the two types of steering vanes that were popular

*Wind-vane self-steering has only been available for thirty years, yet the devices have revolutionized cruising. With a vane to steer us across oceans, now couples and small crews have access to the most remote and lovely cruising grounds in the world. The servo-pendulum-driven unit above is now the dominant type worldwide. (Courtesy Scanmar Marine.)*

all through the seventies and eighties and that steered thousands of sailors around the world. Both types—those that steer via the boat's main rudder and those that steer with an auxiliary rudder—have proven to be efficient in sailing conditions over 5 knots of apparent wind and on any sailing angle except, possibly, power reaching.

The first type is the horizontal-axis, servo-driven gear: Aires, Monitor, Gunning, Atom's, Sailomat (modern version), Fleming, Navik and Saye's Rig. Like the early Hasler gear, these devices rely on wind direction for trim and on a servo-blade attached to the main rudder for steering. Of these, only the Monitor, Sailomat, Fleming and Saye's Rig were still in production in 1991. Gunning, with which Claire Francis had become the first woman to sail across the North Atlantic east to west, had gone out of business, despite being an excellent device and inexpensive to boot. The Aires, which Britisher Nick Franklin developed into the best servo-type gear of its day, ceased production in 1990. And in 1990 the French Atom's rig, which has made dozens of circumnavigations, particularly on the sterns of smaller boats, ceased production.

*The Aires, shown here folded up, long was the favorite among European offshore sailors. The gear went out of production in 1990, but used Aires gears and spare parts are still available.*

The survivors are all good units. Most popular worldwide is the Monitor, manufactured by Scanmar Marine in Sausalito, California. Hans Berwall, who spent several years cruising about the world, knows self-steering as well as any man in the business. The all-stainless-steel Monitor is his refinement of the basic design ideas in devices, such as the Gunning and Aires. The Monitor has a horizontal-axis wind vane that directs the angle of a servo-blade in the water, which then applies pressure on steering lines rigged to the tiller or wheel of the main rudder. Constructed of stainless tubing, the unit is light, very strong and resistant to corrosion. Several years ago Berwall incorporated an improvement to the unit in the form of a kick-up joint in the paddle shaft. This permits you to leave the paddle out of the water when not in use and will save the paddle from loss or bending if it should strike a log in the water.

Similar in concept to the Monitor but with a different execution, the Fleming is an Australian gear that began to catch on worldwide following the 1982–83 BOC Singlehanded Round The World Race, when several of the racers switched to the Fleming after being disappointed with their existing vanes on the leg to Sydney. Like the Monitor or Aires, the Fleming is driven by a horizontal-axis vane that operates a servo-blade in the water that in turn drives the main rudder via steering lines. Because the unit is compact and has a long rudder shaft, it has been engineered with heavy-gauge stainless steel and large bearings. It is a robust unit and has proven itself on numerous occasions in the Southern Ocean.

A smaller and lighter variation on the servo-type of vane is the Navik. It operates on the same basic principles as the Monitor, but has several unique differences. While the power of the servo-blade is used to steer the main rudder, the servo itself is controlled by a small trim tab linked to the vane. The unit is sensitive and will continue to steer when the breeze dies to almost nothing. The units have been in production for many years and have been proven on extensive voyages. Because of its size and weight, the Navik is often chosen for use in boats under 35 feet.

The Sailomat, built in Sweden and designed by Stelan Knoos, is a light and elegant variation on the Montior-Fleming theme. The horizontal-axis, servo-driven unit that Sailomat is now manufacturing is a second-generation design. The first generation, which we have aboard *Clover*, was a horizontal-axis vane with a servo-paddle that drove an auxiliary rudder. The unit was excellent, but too expensive

*The Monitor, which has become the leader among vanes, is built of stainless steel and has the capability to kick up when not in use. Like the Aires, the Monitor has the ability to steer yachts up to 50 feet long.*

to build. So a new model, which drives the boat through lines to the main rudder, was designed. The unit is light, well designed and expertly manufactured. It has proven to be simple to install and very sensitive in light breezes.

The second type of vane depends upon an auxiliary rudder to steer the boat. The rudder can be driven by a trim tab on the trailing edge of the auxiliary rudder or by a servo that trails in the water aft of the rudder. Also, both vertical- and horizontal-axis vanes are used in these systems. The argument for this second type of wind vane is the security a second rudder offers offshore sailors. Should the main rudder become damaged, you can sail the boat under the auxiliary alone. Also, with a second rudder mounted on the stern, usually well aft of the main rudder, the vane has to exert less effort to steer the boat. Less effort translates into less wear and tear and potentially more reliable steering.

That said, and having lived for many thousands of miles with the Sailomat, which has an auxiliary rudder driven by a servo-blade, we've learned that the auxiliary-rudder devices induce more drag—up to half a knot more in *Clover*—than will the simpler servo-blades of the Monitor and Fleming.

The Autohelm may be the most widely sold unit worldwide. It is sold by Scanmar Marine and should not be confused with the electronic autopilots marketed under the same name. The device is rigged with a vertical-axis vane that turns a simple trim tab on the auxiliary rudder's trailing edge. The tab deflects the rudder, which then steers the boat. Were you to construct the simplest-possible self-steering for an outboard rudder on a cruising boat, you would use this same principle. The beauty of the Autohelm is its simplicity. If it has drawbacks, they would be a lack of power, vulnerability in a seaway and the inability to retract the rudder when motoring or using the autopilot.

The RVG vane steering unit is very similar to the Autohelm. Like the Autohelm, it relies on a vertical-axis vane to operate the trim tab, which in turn drives the rudder. Well engineered but expensive, the RVG is not seen as often today in the offshore fleet as it was ten years ago.

The WindPilot is the only remaining European device that uses the auxiliary-rudder system. The German-made rig is a knockoff of the old Sailomat 3040, although it is not as elegantly engineered as the original Swedish unit. The WindPilot has a horizontal-axis vane that operates a servo-blade, which then drives the rudder. The WindPilot is a large and powerful device that is designed to work on larger boats. Although expensive, it may be the only unit with an auxiliary rudder that can be counted on to steer boats over 20 tons or vessels of 50 feet or more.

The last vane in this category to consider for ocean sailing is the Hydrovane, an English unit that has been in production for fifteen

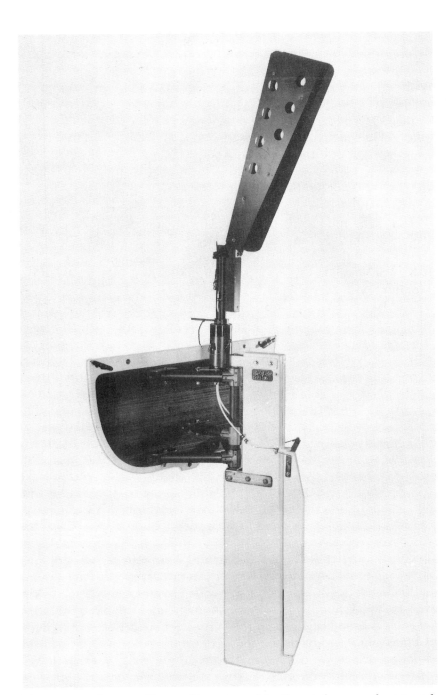

*Vane gear with an auxiliary rudder, operated by the wind vane and a trim tab, provide solid self-steering and the bonus of a spare rudder. The Autohelm shown above is a simple and robust unit that has proven itself around the world.*

years and has proven itself over many thousands of ocean miles. The vane has a horizontal axis that drives a neat and finely engineered gear unit. The rudder is driven by a trim tab that is large and strong enough to work successfully in most conditions.

No matter which type of vane you decide is right for your boat and your style of cruising, it is important to choose an installation that will be reliable and strong. The forces of the sea, particularly the strains put on a rudder and paddle by large beam seas, can crumple light gear and tear loose vanes that have not been very securely attached to the transom. Considering that you will be spending between $2,000 and $4,000 for the device, it is only prudent to make sure it is well attached to the boat.

Finally, you have to make sure that the vane you choose is right for your boat. Lighter units and those with auxiliary rudders tend to work best on smaller and medium-sized boats—up to 45 feet or so. Larger and heavier boats will need to have the power of the servo-blade to match the power of the rudder when things get rough. Of the vanes available, the Fleming and the Monitor are presently the most used; they both have the engineering, the sea time and the power to handle boats up to 20 tons and 50 feet, given that the boats are well balanced and easily steered with the main rudder.

## WIND VANES FOR LARGER BOATS

There has never been designed a commercial wind vane that will steer boats of 55 and 60 feet. The weight of the boats, the sheer speeds and forces involved, have always tended to overpower the Aires- and Monitor-type vanes, although these have long been known as the best of the units available for the job.

The other options on the market include the WindPilot discussed above and the Saye's Rig. The Saye's Rig uses a vertical-axis vane to drive a trim tab that is linked directly to the trailing edge of the main rudder. On boats with outboard rudders, or those too large for mounting a servo-type vane, the Saye's Rig offers a simple solution. Although not as powerful as a servo-type, the trim-tab system offers sufficient force to turn most vessels. On boats up to 60 feet or so, it can be adapted to most conventional rudders.

*Devising a system for wind-vane steering in larger boats has long been a challenge to those who sail in vessels over 50 feet. The Saye's Rig above is a simple system that works the main rudder. It is driven by a large vertical-axis vane. Although the device is large, the installation of the Saye's Rig is simple and the principles involved in transferring wind direction to rudder position well tried.*

Yet if your boat is too large to accommodate a commercial unit, it is possible to fit a custom vane and to have real success with it. Australian Alan Lucas, who has earned a reputation as an innovative and experienced cruising sailor in Australia and the Pacific, has done some innovative work in the area of vanes for larger boats. His design ideas seek to gain power by increasing the size of the vane, fixing the servo and rudder well aft, where they will have the most effect, and by moving the vane itself from side to side so that it is always in clear air. Several of these have been fitted onto larger cruising boats, and results are moderately good. Each has been designed to fit the boat by the owner, so there is no fixed pattern to go from. Suffice it to say, if you understand the principles of how the vane should work, you should be able to develop a vane for your boat that can steer in most conditions.

One of the most innovative vanes I've ever seen is aboard Bob and Sylvia Wells's 60-foot ketch *Sylvia*. Bob and Sylvia have been cruising since the late 1960s, and their *Sylvia* is a Salthouse design, New Zealand–built boat that is both heavy and powerful. At the time she was built (and now), there were no commercial units that could be counted on to steer the boat. Moreover Bob was concerned that a vane unit mounted on the stern was vulnerable to damage from waves, other boats and docks.

His approach, since he was building his boat from the keel up, was to design a self-steering unit that was integral with the hull. His system, which is based on a horizontal-axis vane operating a trim tab on an auxiliary rudder, is unique and very efficient. The auxiliary rudder is hung on a freestanding rudder post just aft of the main rudder. Because the boat has a full-keel, attached-rudder configuration, the auxiliary rudder fits neatly under the counter stern and is well below the water all the time. You can barely see the rudder unless you are right alongside the boat. To reduce strain on the rudder post, the whole rudder assembly can swivel 360 degrees, therefore always being able to feather, no matter what is happening to the boat.

The trim tab is positioned on struts about 18 inches aft of the trailing edge of the rudder, where it will have a maximum torque for a minimum applied force. The narrow vertical trim tab is operated by the horizontal-axis vane on deck, via a sleeve that fits neatly over the main rudder post.

The key to the efficiency of the device is the way the vane drives the trim tab. The vane is mounted on the weather stern rail (and shifted at every tack or jibe to the opposite side), where it always has clear air. The vane drives a simple fan belt on a pulley, which in turn drives a shaft, which leads to the rudder post and drives the trim tab.

If it sounds like Rube Goldberg gone cruising, it isn't. The Wells's vane has steered *Sylvia* many, many thousands of miles, including a west-about circumnavigation. The device is designed specifically for the boat and would not work as well on other types of hull designs. The importance, however, of what Bob and Sylvia did with the vane steerer is the willingness they demonstrated to apply known principles to a new application. Owners of other large boats, as Alan Lucas has also proven, can do likewise with good results.

## AUTOPILOTS

In the offshore fleet of cruising boats, wind vanes are still the work-horses used on long passages. Yet, more and more, mechanical au-topilots are being used. And, for coastal cruising, it is rare today to see a vane. The variety of autopilots now available, the low relative cost of modern units and the high reliability have made the old "Iron Mike" the choice of many sailors.

Aboard *Clover* the addition of an autopilot has changed our ap-proach to sailing. While we used to use the vane even for short hops in any conditions we might be in, we found that we still had to hand-steer on short coastal runs or when motoring. Over the thousands of miles we have sailed we would have steered approximately 15 percent of the time. That's not much. But in many instances it was too much, particularly when the weather was poor and we'd rather be tucked away under the dodger while on watch.

With the autopilot we only steer in and out of harbor or when we are day-sailing along the coast with friends who get a kick out of handling the helm. We leave the wind vane disengaged unless we are headed off on a long run and leave the work to the tireless little electrical beast. For our purposes an efficient vane that can steer well in most conditions—rough weather especially—is very neatly com-plemented by the autopilot.

Choosing an autopilot is not easy. There are several technical choices you will have to make as you seek the right pilot for the job. The first is the power the pilot will deliver to the rudder. Most of the units on the market use small electrical motors (approximately ⅛ to ¼ horsepower) that then drive either a screw actuator or a chain-link drive to the main rudder. Or, if the unit uses an hydraulic actuator, an hydraulic cylinder-arm transfers the drive force to the quadrant.

In either case the power delivered to the main rudder will be sufficient to drive the boat in moderate conditions. Yet in larger boats (over 45 feet), even the larger ¼-hp units will have trouble holding the helm in rough, beam seas. The boat will be hit by a wave, will begin to round up and the pilot will have to struggle to swing the boat back on course. The solution then is first to install the most powerful autopilot possible for the size of your boat and second to make sure you balance the helm and even depower the sails a bit when the seas and wind pick up.

There are units on the market that pack up to ½ horsepower. Designed for commercial vessels, these are rugged and reliable. But they are also bulky and expensive. If you have the room and the budget, such units will serve you well.

As a rule of thumb, you will find that ⅙ horsepower will be sufficient in boats up to about 40 feet. Under 30 feet you can employ the smaller units, and above 40 feet you will do well to seek out an autopilot that packs at least ¼ horsepower. Also, you should estimate your needs not on the average use but on the high-end use, those times when the seas are running and you are slewing down them at hull speed. If you want your autopilot to steer in those conditions, it will have to be powerful.

Autopilots do what you have told them to do: steer a certain course. They do this by comparing a given course with the electronic course they receive from the integral-flux-gate compass. The simplest devices simply measure the difference and alter the rudder angle to compensate. Yet sophisticated pilots will do a lot more, such as adjust the helm for sea state and yaw, increase or decrease the rudder angle and accept and process information from other instruments on board.

The sea state or yaw control essentially adjusts the response of the control-head sensors to compensate for lumpy seas and an irregular motion. Instead of attempting to adjust the boat's course every time a beam sea rolls under the boat, putting it off course for a moment, the sea-state control will delay the rudder response for a second or two. If the boat swings back on course, no response will be needed. If the boat fails to fall back onto course, then the rudder is applied. As units increase in complexity and price, the ability to adjust the sea-state control accurately will increase. On some units you will be able to dial in your own setting for whatever sea conditions you find.

The ability to adjust the pilot for rudder angle accomplishes two necessary tasks. First, the unit must be tuned to your boat's rudder. With an efficient spade rudder situated well aft, a little rudder goes a long way. Too much throw in the autopilot will cause the boat to zig and zag like a slalom skier. Yet on old-fashioned designs with long keels and low-aspect rudders, insufficient rudder angle will delay the response and cause the boat to wander slowly all over the ocean, never quite catching up with the impulses coming from the flux-gate compass. To reach a happy medium, the rudder-angle adjustment has to be set to your boat's steering characteristics. On the more sophisticated units, rudder angle can be measured and controlled by the control head, while on simpler and less expensive units the angle is gauged only by the swing of the compass. Being able to adjust rudder angle manually will allow you to get the best working relationship between the control head and the actual steering device, the rudder.

Another aspect of rudder-angle control is the rate at which the pilot turns the rudder boat and how well it senses the rate of change in the boat's course. If the pilot only turns at one speed, you will find that it will have a hard time responding to sudden course shifts as the boat tries to round up in a bad quartering sea. In these conditions you want the pilot to think and act quickly before the boat has had a chance to broach. Moreover, if the pilot cannot adjust its speed for the rate of change in the boat's course, once it has driven the boat back toward its course, it will continue to oversteer in the other direction. This will set up oscillation and a meandering course across the ocean. Almost all modern units have a way of compensating for rudder angle. And many have built-in sea-state adjustments. Yet only in the more advanced pilots will you find an adjustment for the rate of course adjustment.

The third quality you will have to evaluate is the ability of the pilot to accept information from other instruments on board, navigation instruments in particular. Most middle and top-of-the-line pilots are fitted with networking ports that will permit a Loran C, SatNav or GPS to be linked directly into the control head. In effect this permits you to set up a series of way points that your autopilot will head for one after another. While complex, such a link directs the pilot automatically to fine-tune your adjustments for set and drift when sailing on the wind and across a current. Not bad. Moreover, if you are sailing shorthanded, the interface will relieve you of navigation and piloting duties while you concentrate on sail shape or lunch.

The installation of the autopilot will have a bearing on its reliability and on it long-term use aboard. Smaller cockpit-mounted units, such as the Autohelm 3000 we have on *Clover*, are the most prone to suffering damage from weather and abuse. A wave in the cockpit or a misplaced step can render the unit inoperable. Yet these simple devices can also pack a lot of power in very small packages. When mounting a pilot in the cockpit, make certain that all electrical connections are well sealed with silicone and that the control-head and drive motors are out of the way and securely bolted in place. If the pilot uses a belt to drive the wheel, the belt should be set tight enough to turn the wheel but loose enough to slip easily when the rudder is broadsided by a wave. Tiller-mounted units can create an unnecessary strain on pintels and gudgeons in the same rough seas. The tiller connection should not be the immovable stainless pin commonly sold with the devices. A better solution is to mount the attachment pin on a thick rubber sleeve that slides down over the tiller. The sleeve will bend slightly as the rudder kicks to a wave and will absorb the strain.

In larger units it is best to keep the control head belowdecks if possible. While most autopilots have been designed to have the control head mounted in the cockpit, exposure to the weather is certain, over time, to create moisture problems. The best solution is to mount the control head below and use a remote-control unit to operate it while in the cockpit.

One of the most common failure points for autopilots directly linked to the main quadrant on the rudder post is at the quadrant itself. Quadrants are made of cast bronze or aluminum and are designed to accept heavy side loads from the steering cables. An hydraulic or screw-activated arm from a powerful drive motor that has been bolted directly to the quadrant can and will shatter the casting in rough going. To alleviate this problem, Edson Corp. has designed a mounting plate that bolts to the quadrant. The drive arm is then attached to the plate, which spreads the drive loads across the whole casting instead at one point.

Although the better models of pilots on the market have been well proven, most are controlled in their control heads by complex circuit boards. These are not easily repaired, at sea or anywhere, so those sailing offshore should carry a spare board or two. Excessive strain on the drive motor, or even the simple failure to shut off the pilot before wrenching over the wheel, can cause the control head to overload, heat up and melt the circuits. It happens.

Of the numerous models of pilots on the market, several stand out. The Robertson, from Norway, has a long-proven history of steering fishing boats and smaller commercial vessels in the North Atlantic and North Sea. The basic commercial unit has been modified for use in cruising boats with new sea-state and rudder-angle controls. Moreover, Robertson has developed a line of electronic instruments that can be interfaced along a main control circuit. For reliability, power and efficiency there are few that stand as tall.

In the cruising fleet Autohelm has proven to be the favorite brand. The model 7000 is widely used by larger boats (over 45 feet), and the 6000 is common in the medium range. The 3000, which has been on the market for many years, is used by many cruising sailors in boats from 30 to 50 feet. We have one friend in the Pacific who uses only the 3000 on his Gulfstar 50. For backup he has a second 3000 in the box, which he has never used in four years of ocean cruising. The newer 4000 is basically the same device as the 3000, yet the wheel mount precludes the safety measure of the slipping belt. We have heard of more than a few 4000s that have melted control boards and burned motors due to excessive strain.

Benmar, Wagner, Alpha and Navico are all brands that are widely used, in most cases with success. Benmar and Wagner stand out as brands that have long histories and many millions of miles of reliable service. Alpha and Navico offer satisfactory pilots that cost less than those of their compatriots.

The case for using an autopilot as the sole means of steering a boat—with a second pilot as backup—is strong. Most cruisers don't spend long periods at sea, where a wind vane shines. Most do not have to worry about the drain on the batteries from a constantly operating pilot. Yet I would not be one to set out for an extended cruise with only an autopilot at the helm. There is always a chance that we could lose our batteries, always the chance that the pilot could burn out, always the chance that something unforeseen could go wrong. When it does, the vane will still be there to handle the helmsman's chores.

We don't plan to steer the boat, so we carry both a vane and an autopilot, with spares for each.

## Further Reading

*Offshore Cruising Encyclopedia,* by Steve and Linda Dashew (Ojai, Calif.: Beowulf Publishing Group, 1991).

# Chapter Five

# THE COMMAND CENTER: NAVIGATION AND COMMUNICATIONS

*Your electronics should suit your sailing needs.*

- ▲ What Navigation Systems Should Do
- ▲ Electronics for Coastal Cruising: Depth, Loran, RDF and Radar
- ▲ Electronics for Offshore Cruising: SatNav and GPS
- ▲ Communications Afloat: VHF, SSB, Ham and EPIRB

Not long ago, during the annual migration of cruising boats from Fiji and Tonga to New Zealand for the southern summer—hurricane season—the airwaves were alive one night with a Mayday call. A Swedish sailor, who had sailed singlehanded from his homeland and covered some 15,000 miles in the previous two years, was in distress. He carried a single sideband radio and was able to reach friends and assistance ashore. People all over the northern region of New Zealand sprang into action.

Radio Keri Keri, which monitors boats at sea in the southwestern South Pacific took the call, and soon a cruising friend who had already arrived in New Zealand's Bay of Islands was on the SSB as well. There was some debate about the seriousness of the Swede's predicament. His engine had quit and he was taking on a bit of water. Moreover, he was tired and panicky. It was decided to call the emergency a Mayday, which precipitated two immediate actions: a fishing vessel 120 miles away was diverted and a New Zealand Air Force Orion was launched. When a Mayday is called, all responding expect the distressed sailor to be prepared to abandon his vessel as soon as help arrives.

The Swede continued to speak with his friend on the radio, and it soon became clear that he not only was having mechanical trouble but he had other troubles as well. His SatNav had quit, so he did not know where he was, having no backup and not having mastered celestial navigation. And, he admitted at one point, he had no coastal charts for New Zealand. He was lost, tired and scared out of his wits.

The fishing boat found the beleaguered sailor eight hours later, having steamed at full speed through the night, burning many hundreds of gallons of fuel. The Orion had picked up the cruising boat as well, and the two rescuers coordinated their efforts. The fishermen asked the Swede if he was ready to abandon his ship. He was not. So two sailors launched a boat and came aboard the yacht, where they spent several hours repairing the engine and plugging the leak.

Once under way, with the Mayday all but forgotten, the Swede carried on talking on the SSB. Radio Keri Keri had declined, at that point, to nurse him any further—following a hail of abuse from the tired sailor. Ashore, the friendly cruiser patiently talked the sailor in, giving him courses and bearings and trying to keep him calm.

On the morning of the second day the SSB went quiet, and the VHF began to chatter with the drama. Now off the heads of the Bay of Islands, the sailor was on the verge of exhaustion and demanding in no uncertain terms that a boat be sent out to tow him in. He kept saying, "There's a rock in front of me. I'm going to hit it unless someone does something."

To his rescue came a local cruising boat, out early for a run up the coast. He came alongside the sailor and gave him a chart of the area. Finally the friend ashore appeared in his own cruising boat, found the sailor and led him into the customs dock in the port of Opua.

All who had heard the saga knew there was something very wrong with the tired sailor's behavior, his Mayday call, his verbal abuse, his lack of preparation, lack of basic skills. Many had known him all the way across the Pacific. It was not surprising, then, that no one turned out to catch his lines when he motored up to the pier.

The event had cost many people dearly. The fishing boat lost a day's fishing and consumed many dollars in fuel. They did the right thing and made no fuss about it. But they should not have been put in a position where they were responding to a Mayday that was not much more than exhaustion and a fussy engine. The Orion's missions cost the taxpayers of New Zealand $76,000. It was no doubt the right thing to launch the plane in the face of a Mayday. It is hard to qualify a Mayday situation over the radio, as any offshore sailor knows. It is best to send the Orion first and ask questions later. A man's life might be at stake. And it was good and noble of the friend ashore to sit up all night and chat patiently on the radio, to take up the slack others wanted no part of, and, finally, to sail out and lead the stray lamb in.

No one doubted the rightness of the response, given the Mayday call. Yet, in the aftermath, everyone involved felt hollow. One of our fellows at sea had failed in a very public way and cast a shadow over all who shared the same cruising pastime on the same ocean.

What went wrong? Three things: First, the solo sailor had failed to set up his navigation systems so that he could find his way safely into port even if he had a mechanical failure; second, he had failed to equip himself with the most basic equipment and charts; and lastly, he had used his powerful high-seas radio to call for ultimate help when all he needed was a good night's sleep.

He was the boy who cried wolf.

It is no wonder that more and more fishermen and coasting commercial skippers fail to hear the bleats of yachtsmen who blunder about on their oceans.

Our command centers—the navigation and communications systems we carry aboard—are our lines of defense against such a failure at sea. How we set up our systems and how we plan to use them, whether coastal sailing or venturing across oceans, is a vital part of preparing a vessel for cruising.

## WHAT NAVIGATION SYSTEMS SHOULD DO

There are so many electronic devices available for us to choose from when outfitting a cruising boat, it can be hard to remember the basics of what we want our navigation instruments to do: help us determine our position. As any sailor who has taken a Power Squadrons course or attended one of the several cruising courses offered by charter

*While we depend upon DR and the basics of coastal navigation, we still find the simplicity and accuracy of GPS—the Magellan seen here—to be a good backup. When planning a navigation system, it is important to assess the technology available in terms of what your real needs will be. If you are sticking to the coastline, the DR is the most important element. Offshore, you will want to talk with the satellite if possible.*

companies and sailing schools will know, the most basic item of navigation is dead reckoning.

Dead reckoning—which is really "ded." reckoning for *deduced*—is your estimated position taken simply from magnetic course and distance run. Everything else—"drift" for the boat's leeway and "set" for the affects of current—are applied to the DR in order to figure your actual ded. position.

All electronic aids and other navigational techniques, such as visual bearings and ranges, are then used to check and improve the position arrived at through ded. reckoning. In other words, your GPS position, automatically updated every second on the liquid-crystal screen, is a backup device for your own manual calculations and not vice versa.

If you take this point of view, then the speedometer, log and compass are the heart of your navigation system, for these are the devices that give you the basic information you need. These need to be of good quality, reliable and accurately calibrated. If your compass gives you erroneous information, you'll never get where you want to be. If your speedo and log are unpredictably wrong, you will not be able to measure your distance run and therefore will find yourself at a loss to know when you will arrive at your next landmark.

This point was made clear to me on one autumn trip I made down the East Coast. Having spent too long behind a desk and too little time on the water for a few years—along with the others I sailed with—we managed to subtract compass variation when we should have added it, and we believed our speedo and log when in fact it had not been calibrated and was in error.

The result was that after twenty-four hours of hard sailing before a brisk northerly wind we were not at all where we should have been or where we thought we were. The RDF was giving very odd readings, and we could not pick up land when we should have. It took some time, but we finally discovered our error and made for the coast of New Jersey on a new heading. Late the following night we picked up a sea buoy that corresponded to our charts, and we struck a course from there to the jetty at Cape May, which was flashing a dim red light.

Using the chart we had on board to find our way into Cape May, we sailed in through the breakwater and turned into the mooring area. Things were not as they appeared on the chart, but they were close enough. It was two in the morning when we tied up alongside a fishing trawler and turned in, satisfied that we had overcome our poor navigation.

We got a rude surprise in the morning. One of our crew went ashore for milk and came back waving a place mat from a local diner. At last we had a positive fix, and we weren't in Cape May at all. We were in fact in Ocean City, Maryland, sixty miles to the south and in a different state. Ouch.

We had misused the compass and trusted a faulty log and counted ourselves lucky to be able to laugh about it later.

With an accurate DR in mind and the knowledge to use a compass and log properly, the navigation systems can then be built upon a sound base. Along the same lines, sailors heading offshore should remember that the use of celestial navigation is not an option but the first level of competence. The boat should be equipped with a serviceable sextant, calibrated and ready to use, and the navigation station should have the Nautical Almanac, sight-reduction tables (H.O. 249 is easiest) and a chronometer set to Greenwich Mean Time (also called UTC) always at hand. Moreover, when setting out on a long coastal run or across an ocean, the navigator should satisfy himself and the crew that given the failure of any and all electronic aids he or she can still fix a position and set a course for a safe landfall.

Once the basic systems are in place, all types of further electronic aids will make the navigator's life easier.

## ELECTRONICS FOR COASTAL CRUISING: DEPTH, LORAN, RDF AND RADAR

When coastal cruising, most navigation is done within sight of land and most of the work you will be doing will involve taking direct information from the landmarks around you. Unlike offshore sailing, you need to be alert all the time to the depth, to your course and to the relative distances between the coast and islands around you. And, unlike offshore navigation, there are usually a variety of different ways to ascertain your position.

Modern charts are so accurate and detailed that the depth of the water beneath your keel can be used easily to check your DR. Twenty years ago, before the advent of Loran and inexpensive radar, the lead line or depth sounder was a key navigational instrument. It was common when making coastal runs, particularly in poor visibility, to set a course along a depth curve and then check progress along the course with frequent soundings. Electronic depth sounders make this job simple. While there are a wide variety of sounders on the market, most of the well-known brands will give extremely accurate readings while you sail along at normal speeds.

The best way to set up a depth sounder is to have the transponder positioned well below the waterline and forward of the keel. The transponder can be mounted through the hull and should be installed level with the waterline. It is common to use a shaped wood block between the outside skin of the hull and the bottom of the transponder to secure the unit in place and to fix it on a level plane. On some modern units the transponder can be mounted inside the fiberglass hull in a sealed oil bath. The sonic impulses travel through the fiberglass without significant interference and can save your having to put yet another hole in the hull.

The best arrangement is to position the main control head and readout—whether digital or analog—at the chart table. The wiring will be simplest here, and the unit can be protected from damage from the environment. The navigator can read soundings while working on the charts and thus has a ready check on where the boat is relative to the bottom. For most areas of coastal sailing a unit that reads to 20 fathoms, or 120 feet, will be sufficient. However, if you will be sailing offshore, it is helpful to have a unit that will read to 50 fathoms or more. When making a landfall, you can often pick up the bottom of the continental shelf—on the East Coast of America and in many regions of Europe—before you see the low-lying shore. Aboard *Clover* we have a Seafarer analog depth sounder that operates on three scales, permitting us to plumb depths from 0 to 360 feet with a high degree of accuracy.

For poking around harbors it makes sense to have a repeater for the sounder in the cockpit. As you work your way close to shore or around known landmarks, you can watch the depth and find the right hole for dropping the anchor. Even in darkness or poor weather an accurate depth sounder in the cockpit will give you an early warning of a shelving bottom and a good indication if you are steering the boat into deep water. Most of the better sounders have depth alarms, which can be helpful while at anchor to warn you if you have swung or dragged into shallow water. Brookes and Gatehouse, Datamarine, Signet, Stowe and many other brands will do the job nicely for you.

Along the coast there is nothing like radar for keeping an eye on landmarks and watching the sea around you for ship traffic. In northern areas, where you can expect fog, radar can mean the difference between sailing and not sailing. In the past few years the prices of radar have come down significantly. It is possible to buy smaller units—Apelco and Furuno, for example—that will have a 16-mile range and all the applications you will need. Moreover, the newer models are quite abstemious with power consumption, so you can use them more often when under sail.

Radar will give you a wide range of information, from distance off—very accurately—to bearings and cross-track information. While you will find that it takes some practice to get the best from your radar, the electronic eye watching out all around you will give you your position relative to real landmarks like nothing else. Although most charts available for North America and the civilized world are kept up-to-date and are very accurate, you will find in some regions of the world—even in island groups not too far from home—that islands are not always where the chart says they ought to be. Electronic aids such as Loran will give you an accurate chart location. But if the chart is wrong, if the buoys have been moved or removed, if storms have altered a harbor entrance, the Loran will be of little help. In such situations the radar will give you the hard facts, gleaned from a real reflection off the landmarks you're seeking.

Radar will also alert you to pending emergencies. Most units today have the ability to set a guard zone around your boat. If you set the zone at 10 miles, which should be just over the horizon, you can then rest assured that any ship that comes your way will be picked up and, once inside the guard zone, the buzzer will alert you to its presence. For those of us who sail with small crews and use autopilots and wind vanes, such a guard zone can be a comfort. It does not remove the responsibility to keep someone on watch and alert through the night. But as a backup and an aid it is invaluable.

While a depth sounder and radar give you empirical information from the real world around you, radio direction finders and Loran give you electronic information from known broadcast points that then must be plotted on your charts. The information you get will only be as good as your receivers and on the charts you then use for plotting.

Still, RDF—particularly in Europe—and Loran are excellent aids to navigation and belong on any well-found coastal cruising boat.

RDF is somewhat old-fashioned. Along the coast of North America hundreds of low-powered marine beacons mark the entrances of harbors, and a few longer-range beacons (120 miles or so) broadcast from light stations and towers at the major ports. More frequent along the coasts are aero beacons at coastal airports, which all have long-range broadcasts and are maintained by the Federal Communications Commission. Between the two types of beacons there are usually two in your vicinity that can be used for cross-bearings. In Europe marine RDF has been refined to a high degree and can be used by coastal boats from Norway to Gibraltar and throughout the Mediterranean with very satisfactory results.

Twenty years ago there were a dozen different receivers on the market, for RDF was used by many sailors. Today there are only a few brands available. Yet as an inexpensive backup to DR and other electronic forms of navigation, RDF has a viable place aboard a cruising boat. Sophisticated units, such as the Brookes and Gatehouse, are high-frequency receivers as well as RDF receivers. The less-expensive models, such as the Ray Jeff, will be good FM and AM receivers as well as RDFs.

Aboard *Clover* we carry the German-made Arienne Automatic Direction Finder, which is a superb model and will give very accurate relative bearings of the chosen frequencies very quickly. Although we carry several other types of electronic devices, we still use the RDF to check our position whenever we find a good group of beacons to choose from. RDF is possibly the least accurate electronic aid. Yet it works well as a homing device when coming into port in poor visibility. As you get close to the beacon, the accuracy of the fix, or line of position, improves.

If you are planing to cruise in Europe, a sophisticated device such as the B&G or the Arienne is well worth the money. For cruising North America and the rest of the world, RDF should be considered a backup that can fill in when other devices have failed. If possible, the RDF should be permanently mounted in the nav. station.

Loran C, which evolved from the old Loran A, is a remarkable navigational aid and has changed the way many of us think about finding our positions as we sail along the coasts. Not only will a good Loran give you your position, in either latitude and longitude or the "time delay" of TD lines, but it will give you your speed over the bottom, course, set and drift and figure courses for you to establish waypoints ahead.

The Loran system, like RDF, is based upon coastal broadcasts on specific frequencies. Each station has a master and a slave broadcast. When the Loran aboard measures the time delay between the two broadcasts, it can fix your position with extraordinary accuracy. The amazing quality of Loran, however, is its repeatability. Once you have entered a correct coordinate for a specific spot on the ocean, you can always return to that spot—with an accuracy of literally several meters. Commercial fishermen often carry two Lorans aboard to ensure that they can find their special fishing grounds or avoid a snag on the bottom that has already claimed a net.

If Loran has a flaw, it is only that it is tricky to use well. It is perfectly possible, while sailing close to shore and in your home waters, to set the Loran's initialization once and then never touch the machine again. It will continue to give you a position, your speed and your course. However, when making longer passages to cruising grounds farther afield, Loran needs to be tweaked and coddled to get the best results.

On the East Coast of the United States, for example, when sailing north to the coast of Maine and farther to New Brunswick, Nova Scotia and Newfoundland, the Loran signal will be affected by land interference and other anomalies. Similarly, when sailing in the Bahamas, the distance from the mainland broadcast stations becomes so great that the signal and the device's ability to measure the time delays decrease in effectiveness. In both cases, without warning, the Loran will begin to give inaccurate positions, which become less and less accurate the farther you go. It is possible to reinitialize the receiver, to adjust the sine-wave adjustment and to adjust the notch filters for better results. Many sailors who frequent the extremes of the coast have discovered the tricks of the Loran trade in these pleasant outposts. And you will find small publications available for both regions to help you make the needed adjustments.

The point, however, is that Loran is a local device that soon loses its accuracy as you leave the mainland coast and populous areas. It is not designed to navigate you to Bermuda or Hawaii or out to the Azores. Moreover, it is not at its best when traveling over land. In the higher regions of large estuaries, such as San Francisco Bay, Loran readings can be out by hundreds of yards, which is too much for comfort. Loran is a marvelous tool and has made coastal piloting much safer and easier. But it should not be used blindly nor trusted implicitly. Among the best units, Trimble, Raytheon and Magnavox stand out. Yet there are many fine units that can be had for bargain prices. Micrologic, Apelco, Navstar and Furuno and others all manufacture Loran receivers that will be reliable and economical.

How you fit out your navigation systems for coastal sailing and cruising will depend in large part on your budget. Assuming you have good compasses and a log already on board, I would next add a depth sounder. Following that, Loran would be next, for it does so many things well. Radar is the next item I would add, for it provides a level of safety that is very appealing. Lastly, the RDF would be included in the list as a backup. When the Loran has gone silly because of land or distance anomalies and the radar is on the blink because the batteries are low, the RDF will be there to help you in.

# ELECTRONICS FOR OFFSHORE CRUISING: SATNAV AND GPS

The great satellite revolution hit the offshore cruising fleet in the mid-1970s when SatNav became available. The technology and the orbiting satellites had been in place for almost a decade before but had been reserved for military use. Once the public was invited to play, it became possible for even amateur navigators to contemplate crossing oceans and offered a new level of safety and security for veteran navigators.

Based upon a series of satellites, the Transit System, which are in polar orbit, the SatNav receiver locates birds overhead, locks onto their signal, and then accepts data from them. The principle is based on the Doppler effect. Basically, the receiver collects the bird's position and then measures the rate of change in the signal as the satellite passes. By calculating this change, the receiver can then fix your position. It's a wonderful technology. However, it is rapidly becoming obsolete. The satellites that offer the data are being replaced by a new system, hence the SatNav receivers we have come to rely upon only have a useful life until about the year 2000.

As of this writing in 1991, there are still excellent SatNav units on the market. In particular Magnavox, Raytheon and Trimble offer receivers with the widest array of functions and the most sophisticated circuitry. Prices have come down, and today it is possible to equip a boat with a device that will have at least eight years of useful service for about the cost of a Loran.

The benefits of SatNav are numerous. Not only will the system give you a position no matter what the weather looks like, it will also interface with many speedometers and logs and flux-gate compasses to give you a constantly updated DR. Simpler units require the DR information to be input manually and therefore are not as useful for ongoing DRs. Yet what you want from the receiver is a position first and foremost. The ongoing DR can always be figured on scrap paper.

The two common complaints offshore sailors make about their SatNavs is the need to initialize the unit every time it is switched on (less expensive units) and the long gaps sometimes found between fixes. The better units mentioned above all have internal batteries that will keep the last fix and other initialization data in memory while the unit is off. And some of the simpler units have the ability to be wired with small 9-volt batteries—use nickel-cadmium for long life and constant voltage—to keep the memory current when not in use. The ability to retain data in memory while shut down is a real plus and should be sought in a new device.

The problem of time lapses between fixes is a frustrating one. It may be coincidence, but it seems that the satellites always go dormant just when you are getting ready for a landfall. In the best of times you can expect a fix just about every hour. In the worst of times we have seen the SatNav go without acceptable satellite fixes for up to six hours. While any navigator accustomed to sailing with only his sextant would find a positive fix every six hours to be almost overkill, those of us who have grown used to instant fixes of Loran and GPS can find the delays positively annoying. It's a matter of perspective.

The real trouble with SatNav is the advent of GPS. In 1991 the major manufacturers of GPS units were crowing that the Global Position System was finally active twenty-four hours a day. Well, almost. In fact the GPS system, which is dependent upon nearly two dozen satellites, is active anywhere between twenty-two and twenty-four hours a day. This is meant to be gradually improved over the years and should be fully functional by late 1992.

Yet even with a brief downtime during the day, GPS receivers do for offshore sailors what Loran C does for coastal navigators: You can now have pinpoint navigation whenever you want it (almost), no matter where you are in the world. Moreover, you can use waypoints, speed and distance information and keep track of your progress through a dozen course changes. Lastly, you'll always have GMT accurately displayed to the nearest one-tenth second.

With a GPS unit you can check your compass and adjust it for deviation. You can check your speedometer and log and set them accurately. You can figure great-circle courses between any two points in the world. And you can have the perverse satisfaction of knowing exactly how far off the world's cartographers are when drawing their navigational charts.

This last point shows up the one cautionary note to be sounded about GPS. In the 12,000 miles I have used my Magellan unit, it has functioned extremely well and always given us positions within yards of where we were. Yet it has also shown that some of our favorite islands are not where they are supposed to be. For example, Stocking Island in the Exuma chain of the Bahamas is fully five miles out of position on the large-scale DMA chart of the area. About the world it is no different. Anchored in Nuku Hiva in the Marquesas, we found that the island was nearly three miles out of plumb with our actual position.

The question: Do you believe the GPS or the chart? We have found that in areas in which there has been little recent survey work, in areas far from the world's busy ports, you should trust the GPS. If you are in a well-traveled region, a region covered by Loran, then it would be wise to trust the chart first and check the GPS.

When setting waypoints in far-flung areas, we take the precaution of assuming the cartographers are at least three miles out in their calculations and place our waypoint that distance or more from the landfall we are seeking. Thus, should we arrive in poor visibility, we won't be lured ashore by our GPS, which does not know the island is not where we thought.

For offshore navigation we carry a sextant and the appropriate tables ready at the chart table. Yet we use them only at the beginning and end of a voyage, first to make sure we remember how and second to check that our electronic positions are accurate. We carry both a SatNav, the old Combi 502, and the Magellan GPS. With both working and both spitting out our position, we have developed a high level of confidence in their reliability.

Among the many units on the market, Raytheon, Trimble, Magnavox and Magellan have been the leaders. Navstar, Micrologic and others have also joined the flood of devices and provide good units at economical prices. GPS units came down significantly in price in 1991. While the prices may continue to drift downward somewhat in the years to come, $1,200 to $1,750 seems to be the threshold for brands that will do all you want them to do.

## COMMUNICATIONS AFLOAT: VHF, SSB, HAM AND EPIRB

The opportunities for sailors to stay in touch with each other and with family and friends ashore have never been better. While it was common in generations past to eschew radios aboard and to sail self-sufficiently into the sunset, today times have changed, radios have changed and shore stations have changed. It is now possible for boats sailing just about anywhere in the world to keep in contact with someone.

Synthesized VHF radios are the workhorses of coastal communications. The VHF is a "very high frequency" radio that sends a clear signal on a very narrow band over a short distance. The limit of the radios is the line of sight, with a little more distance possible in good conditions. That means you can count on talk over a range of 20 to 40 miles, with an occasional contact as much as 60 miles away. In our experience just about every cruising boat we've met, either along the coast of North America or out about the world, has a VHF aboard. The little radios are useful for boat-to-boat communications in harbors, for talking with marinas, harbor controls in foreign ports and for contacting ships at sea. In many far-flung harbors where cruising boats collect, the fleet will initiate a cruising network every morning so that sailors can share information on local customs and help each other solve problems. Closer to home, the VHF is the phone. With it you can contact one of the many marine operators along the U.S. coast and place a telephone call virtually anywhere in the world.

The choice of radios is wide and varied. You can get radios that will scan frequencies, radios that have remote speakers and radios that have a "dual" function for monitoring two frequencies at once. Virtually all the radios on the market today are fully synthesized, meaning they can broadcast and receive on all legal frequencies and do not require crystal chips for tuning into special or local stations.

A VHF should be mounted in a spot where it can be used easily and heard from the cockpit. We once had a scare on Chesapeake Bay when we were making port after dark. A commercial tug pushing a fuel barge was coming at us and was so lit up that we could not see his running lights to determine his course. We kept altering our course to avoid him but still we seemed to be on a collision course. We had our engine running and the VHF mounted down below in the enclosed nav. station, where it could not be heard from the cockpit. As it turned out, the tug's skipper had been trying to contact us as we converged to tell us of his course and explain what he was doing. Unable to hear him, we steered the wrong way to avoid him at first, and only when a collision was imminent did we realize he was turning toward us and we were then able to avoid him. But only by a hundred yards or so. Had we been able to hear the VHF over the thrumming of the engine, the near disaster could have been averted. Needless to say, soon thereafter we fixed a remote speaker in the companionway, where we could monitor calls from anywhere on the boat.

The dual function is useful as well. When cruising with friends, we often will select a channel for our own use—68 or 72 in the States and 06 overseas work well—and keep the radio tuned to that frequency. Yet we like to keep Channel 16 on as well; in fact we legally must keep it open. With the dual function we can monitor both channels at the same time. Lastly the efficiency of the VHF will depend upon the antenna. The choice is either a 6-decibel or a 9-decibel antenna. The 6-db models will give you a better signal at short range, while the 9-db will give you a longer throw.

If VHF is the everyday workhorse of communications, a high-frequency marine radio that covers all the high-seas marine bands on single sideband (SSB) is the radio of choice offshore and about the world. You need only your simple VHF station license to apply for an SSB license, and with it you can speak to other vessels or shore stations thousands of miles away. In the past few years SSB has become increasingly popular among offshore cruisers. In the Caribbean, Bahamas and throughout the South Pacific, regular SSB nets for cruising boats keep you abreast of what's going on in the region and offer those interested a regular system for staying in touch with friends. While the SSB nets are occasionally abused by overzealous sailors who dominate a net, on the whole SSB nets work well and provide both a safety net for voyagers and an electronic coffee klatch for social chit-chat.

There are lots of different radios to choose from. The ICOM 7000 and the Kenwood high-seas radio are two of the most popular. Straight-forward SSBs, these can be programmed to a wide variety of frequencies and have 100 watts or more of output power. The benefit of preselected channels is the ability to dial up an emergency frequency quickly. Moreover, when chatting with friends, it is often desirable to find a clear channel, which is made easier with preselected channels. Finally, when you use duplex frequencies—separate channels for broadcasting and receiving—which are the norm for ship-to-shore work, you will find it much simpler to work a range of channels if you have them already stored in memory.

The downside of units with preselected channels is the difficulty you have in adjusting and fine-tuning a frequency. If, because of propagation, you need to shift a few hertz in one direction to clear a signal, you can't do it easily when the channels are selected from memory. A simple, old-fashioned tuning dial works better. Moreover, if you want to scan through a wide range of bands looking for the BBC news or to find a new channel to work, you simply can't do it with preselected channels. In particular, if you want to listen in on the ham nets around the world to pick up weather and other infor-mation, you will need a way to scan bands in a quick and easy way.

For high-seas work many sailors are choosing to use radios that have a full capability to receive and broadcast on all frequencies, including the designated ham channels. Radios such as the ICOM 735, which is marketed as a full-frequency transceiver but dedicated to ham broad-cast, can be adapted by a knowledgeable technician to broadcast on all frequencies. The hitch is that it is illegal to broadcast on ham and some other frequencies without the appropriate licenses. Such radios have infinite tuning dials and can be set for operation on both simplex (single channel operation) and duplex.

For ship-to-shore communications, SSB can be used to make phones calls via shore stations around the United States (WOO in New York, WOM in Miami, WLO in the Gulf of Mexico and KMI in San Francisco). While expensive, these phone calls are a simple and ef-ficient way to maintain contact with those ashore. Moreover, if you want to transact business while at sea or far from home, you must use commercial frequencies; it is illegal to conduct business affairs on the ham bands. Finally, if you set up an account with ATT (dial 1–800-SEA-CALL), those ashore can leave a message for you with the high-seas operator. Several times a day—the same time the station gives high-seas weather—a list of vessels for whom there is traffic will be called.

The last and possibly most important benefit of a marine SSB for ocean cruisers is the ability to tune into a range of weather forecasts around the world. In the North Atlantic, Norfolk Coast Guard offers excellent forecasts via WMN radio. For the Caribbean and Gulf of Mexico, WLO gives the best weather, and in the North Pacific, KMI gives the best weather picture. Once you have become accustomed to copying down the information given by these channels, you will find you can quickly get a good synopsis of the weather for thousands of miles around you.

For more detailed weather, however, the ability to receive and study weather maps via the international system of fax broadcasts is the best defense against getting caught in inclement conditions. A dedicated weather fax receiver and recorder has its own high-seas receiver and will collect and print weather maps for you. In our experience the quality of the receivers in weather faxes is not as good as it is in your SSB. Thus it makes some sense to be able to link your fax to the SSB for reception. A weather fax will cost anywhere from $1,500 to $3,000. Yet if you carry a portable personal computer aboard, such as a laptop, it is possible to adapt a simple radio modem to your SSB and collect the fax information in your computer, where you can view it on the screen, keep it in memory and print it out on your printer. These systems are available for most computers from D. F. Crane (710 13th St., #209, San Diego, Calif. 92101) for approximately $100.

Aboard *Clover* we did not intend to cruise with a high-frequency radio. We did not want to have our days cluttered with networks and schedules, nor did we want to rely on outside help should we get ourselves into trouble. Looking back, such an attitude seems a bit old-fashioned and even arch. We had the good fortune to acquire an excellent ICOM 720 before we left, so we installed it and set up the antenna, never really intending to use it except in emergencies. Well, two years later I doubt we would go to sea without it. Not only does the radio enable us to receive a wide range of weather information— which we can also receive on our two other shortwave receivers— but we can also keep in touch with our friends out and about the cruising grounds and we can place the occasional call home via the high-seas operators. It's the modern age, and albeit reluctantly, we've joined it.

Ham radio is still used by many cruising folk out about the world. For coastal sailing, ham really has little use other than as a delightful hobby that can double as a fun way to contact family friends ashore via "phone patches" through helpful hams ashore. Yet, in the offshore-cruising grounds, there are a wide array of ham maritime mobile nets that enable you to communicate with a far-flung community that is always eager to chat and can often be useful. These days ham might well be regarded as a hobby as well as a way to communicate with fellow sailors. Most cruising hams also monitor the SSB nets, so you don't need ham to reach them. But if you want to take part in the hobby and make friends in the countries you are going to visit, then ham is a great way to do it.

If you are trying to decide whether to get your ham license, it is good to remember that you don't need to be a ham to have a very productive and sociable time with your SSB. But the ham can save you money—calling countries where phone patches are allowed—and will introduce you to a segment of the cruising fraternity that you might otherwise miss. On the whole the newcomers to the cruising fleet stick to SSB, whereas the veterans tend to migrate to the sanctity of the ham bands.

The last radio to think about is the last radio you will use should you get into serious trouble: the Emergency Position Indicating Radio Beacon or EPIRB. Although you hope you will never have to flip the switch on an EPIRB other than to test it, any sailors heading out, even for coastal runs, should seriously consider carrying at least one last-ditch calling radio aboard.

For commercial vessels registered in the United States EPIRBs are required equipment. Moreover, in 1990 the Coast Guard decreed that all commercial vessels carry the new 406-frequency radios, which are designed to operate through the joint U.S.-Russian COSPAS/SAR-SAT satellite systems. Because it is the law for fishermen and all others who make their living on the sea to carry the devices, a wide variety of 406 EPIRBs are on the market. They are expensive, ranging in price (in 1991) from $1,500 to $10,000.

Yet the new 406 units have corrected some of the basic flaws in the range of Class-A and B EPIRBs that had been on the market prior to 1990. The original system was based on the ability of overflying aircraft and satellites to receive a distress message from a ship at sea and then provide searchers with a homing beacon. The trouble was that more than 90 percent of all recorded distress signals were false alarms. The Coast Guard and AMVER rescue-at-sea system, which coordinates commercial ships for rescue missions, were frustrated by the inability to tell which calls were real and which weren't. Also, it became apparent that many of the units on the market a few years ago did not comply with FCC standards and may not do the job. Moreover the system was not worldwide, with large gaps in the South Pacific, Indian Ocean and South Atlantic.

The new units are designed to communicate directly with the satellites and carry a detailed message about the boat in distress and its location. Unlike the earlier system, the 406 message is held in the satellite's memory and is broadcast to shore stations, where the distress call is then relayed to the Coast Guard, which in turn organizes search-and-rescue efforts. The system is worldwide and offers a much higher degree of safety for mariners than is provided by the older models.

That said, the old Class A and B, EPIRBs, which retail for as little as $350, are better engineered today than they were in 1990. The regulations that brought in the 406 devices also set more stringent regulations for the standard sets, thereby improving performance and reliability. Whether you choose to sail with a 406 for worldwide coverage or the less-expensive models, it is only prudent to carry some form of last-resort communications.

What is the ideal communications system for a coastal-cruising boat? A good VHF that can monitor two stations and can be used from the cockpit is the basic choice. Following that, coastal sailors would do well to carry a basic Class-B EPIRB.

For offshore sailors, in addition to VHF and basic EPIRB, it is wise to carry a high-frequency radio that can monitor the full range of marine and ham frequencies and can broadcast effectively on international ship-to-ship and ship-to-shore frequencies. Additionally, if you are venturing far and wide, a weather fax or computer link is very helpful and a 406-grade EPIRB will offer the last measure of security available.

In the old days it was common to sail alone on the high seas and put one's faith in the boat and your own skill. Today that is no longer the case. With communications so available and so reliable, it seems to me that any sailor who can afford to fit out his vessel with high-seas radio and EPIRB should do so, even if these modern devices are saved solely for emergencies. Who knows, like us, you may come to enjoy being part of the world radio networks.

## Further Reading

*The Big Book of Marine Electronics,* by Frederick Graves (Camden, Me.: International Marine Publishing, 1986).

*Offshore Cruising Encyclopedia,* by Steve and Linda Dashew (Ojai, Calif.; Beowulf Publishing Group, 1991).

*Safety at Sea,* by George Day (New York: G. P. Putnam's Sons, 1991).

## Chapter Six

# ENGINEERING AND ENERGY SYSTEMS

*Plan your systems to meet your needs and wants.*

- ▲ Figuring Energy Needs and Battery Capacity
- ▲ Engine-Driven Battery Charging
- ▲ Simple On-Board Systems: Three Variations
- ▲ On-Board Systems for Larger Boats
- ▲ Living with the Diesel
- ▲ Alternative Sources of Energy

One evening in Tahiti a few couples joined us for a stroll to one of the hotels to watch an evening of Tahitian dancing and to while away a few hours at a tropical bar by the beach. All of us had been living aboard for a year or more, and as is often the way, the evening's conversation turned to technical things, and in particular to amps. What did we all use for batteries? What were our daily loads? How did we charge our batteries? And so on.

As we were walking home, men and women together still embroiled in the conversation, LaVonne, who had been away cruising with her

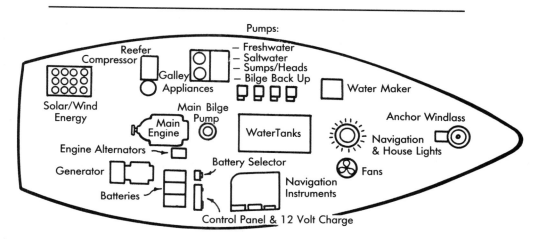

*Modern cruising boats have become complex. The systems on boats can create a wide range of creature comforts, all of which can make sailing and living aboard more enjoyable. But in the process of adding systems to the boat, it is important to measure the consumption of energy with the boat's ability to keep those systems going.*

friend, Tom, for quite a while piped up with a smile and said, "Do you guys remember when groups of friends like this used to talk about politics and clothes and schools? Now all we talk about is boat gear."

We all laughed. That was a different life. For us now the real world was one intimately linked to amps. They drive just about everything on board and cause more reason for concern than just about any element of cruising and living aboard. While living aboard brings the problem of generating and using amps clearly into focus, the basic engineering systems and the gear we run off our batteries is a fact of owning and using any modern boat, whether weekend cruising along the coast or venturing far and wide.

In the offshore fleet most boats have evolved fairly complex systems for running all the on-board gear we have deemed necessary and worthwhile. Gone, it seems, are the days of simplicity, days of kerosene lights, sextants, windup chronometers, and manual freshwater pumps. Even the simplest cruising boats these days have pressure hot-and cold-running water, electronics for navigation, electric bilge pumps and a variety of running and houselights—all of which require amps.

In larger new boats, over 45 feet let's say, it is common to see a wide array of on-board systems come as part of the package. Builders are selling comfort and convenience as much as they are selling a seaworthy hull and an efficient sailing system. Therefore you will find the boat loaded with switch-on electrical devices, from air-conditioning to multiple freshwater pumps to multizone stereo. All of it makes life aboard better. Yet, too often, the engineers who have written the specifications for such boats have neglected to allow for an ample margin in the battery reserves. It may be necessary to charge several hours a day or to run the generator when you'd rather be sitting in a quiet anchorage. It is important, even with large and famous brands of cruising boats, to make certain that you and your engine are not slaves to the batteries because too little capacity has been provided.

Figuring out what your needs are for amps on a daily basis and then coordinating your systems accordingly can make the difference between happy and carefree cruising and the constant problem of charging batteries and keeping up the engineering status quo. And while you can create an engineering and energy system aboard as complex as you like, it makes sense to keep in mind that on a cruising boat, complexity automatically increases maintenance: there's no such thing as a free amp.

That's why, in a discussion of on-board systems that includes everything from refrigeration to pumps, we'll approach it from the energy required to run the systems and how best to plan for successful and trouble-free systems.

## FIGURING ENERGY NEEDS AND BATTERY CAPACITY

The heart of the question is how much energy you need and want to consume on a daily basis. Once you arrive at that number, you can determine how best to resupply the batteries that then can power the boat. There are two general approaches to running your on-board systems: one employed and perfected by companies running large bareboat charter fleets and another that has evolved in the offshore fleet.

The bareboat approach strives for simplicity and reliability aboard boats that are heavily used and that will be running the main engine everyday. This active use means that all the basic systems can be run off the main engine and that battery capacity can be kept to a minimum while use can be at a maximum.

The live-aboard approach allows for days on end without actively charging the batteries and therefore requires not only an active ap-proach to charging but a passive system as well. Plus, in such a system, battery capacity plays a key role. Aboard a live-aboard boat, or one with many on-board systems, you can never have too many amps.

To figure your daily needs, you have to do some detective work. Every electrical item, from the lights to the fridge to the Loran, will require a certain current draw. To estimate your needs, measure the use in amperes per hour. For lights or other devices rated in watts, add the average number used daily, divide that total by 12 (for the 12-volt system), and the result will be the hourly amperage use. Mul-tiply that times the number of hours of use, and you will have the daily draw.

That total has to be replaced, and to have a system that is reliable and long-lived, it should not place too great a drain on the batteries before recharging. We use the bareboat system, which means we plan to be moving and motoring quite often so that we rely on our alternator for all of our power. It works fine, but were we to live aboard at anchor for a time, we would need to supplement the alternator with wind power or solar power.

The batteries take the brunt of all the work done by electrical systems. There are several options when selecting batteries. The basic deep-cycle marine batteries available from Surrette and others can work fine. For larger boats, 4D-size batteries, which rate at about 100 amps, are the standard. Yet there are many who swear by 100-amp golf-cart batteries, which are designed to take a deep discharge and to be put through repeated cycles. The new gelcell batteries built by the German firm Sonnenschein are sealed deep-cycle batteries that have a long life, can be recycled as many as 1,200 times and do not emit poison gas when submerged. These cost about twice as much as a basic lead-acid battery, but can give years more service.

Basic lead-acid batteries are based around lead plates immersed in a sulfuric-acid bath. In general a battery should accept a full charge of 12.8 volts and will discharge quite rapidly to 12.5 volts under moderate use. It will then slowly feed power out at 12.5 volts until it reaches approximately 80 percent of its rated charge at approximately 12 volts. The battery will then begin to lose power a bit more rapidly and will discharge to 50 percent of its total capacity of approximately 11 volts. Below that level the battery quickly runs out of power and lights will dim, some electronics will not operate, and the battery itself will be damaged.

A good-quality lead-acid battery should be good for 500 50-percent discharges and 750 or more 80-percent discharges. A battery that has been run flat will never again hold its rated capacity, nor will it maintain 12.5 volts for more than a short while. Gelcells, however, can be run dead flat and be brought back slowly with repeated slow charges.

With that in mind you should figure your daily working loads as 60 to 80 percent of your capacity. If your daily load is 50 amps, then your working bank of batteries—probably the house bank—should hold at least 200 amp/hours. If your daily draw is 100 amps, you need to double the size of your bank to 400 amp/hours. By working with this margin of reserve, you will prolong the lives of your batteries and will maintain a ready reservoir of amps to last an extra day or two if need be.

If you have the room aboard to carry extra batteries, to increase your reserves to five or six times the average daily draw, you will be in even better shape. The use of gelcells will be a help. But gelcells and lead-acid batteries should not be wired together, for they maintain slightly different ambient charges and will set up a current that can slowly deplete both batteries.

Or you can take a more expensive route and install nickel-cadmium batteries, which will accept deep discharges for years without renewal. Lastly, if you are building a boat from scratch, you can provide room for the ultimate battery bank, which is composed of huge 2-volt gelcells wired into 12-volt configurations. Two-volt batteries have huge plates, isolated into small groups—the most efficient way to store electricity— and thus will give you the greatest performance, the longest reserve and the most charging cycles, all at a vast price.

For most sailors, however, plain deep-cycle batteries of the type used in golf carts or those sold as marine batteries will suffice. These will have to be renewed from time to time. For coastal-cruising boats used on weekends and during summer cruises, if the batteries are well charged during the season and then stored with a full charge in a cool, dry place all winter, you can expect to get five seasons from a set. For those living aboard, if you rarely discharge past 75 percent of capacity, you will find that you can get four good years from the batteries. If you have a smaller battery bank and regularly discharge to 50 percent or lower, you will find eighteen months to two years will be all you will get from lead-acid batteries, and two years or slightly more from gelcells.

# ENGINE-DRIVEN BATTERY CHARGING

A science and a small industry have grown up around the somewhat mysterious realm of battery charging. Among the experts there is little agreement as to what is the best system, as they have all developed charging techniques that are supposed to be better than the rest. No doubt there is an ultimate solution, and it will not be the same for everyone.

Batteries do best when they are put through the normal discharge-and-charge cycle. A battery left discharged will gradually die whereas a battery that is always kept at full charge will gradually lose its deep-cycle capability. The trick to getting reliable performance is to match your charging rate with your usual engine usage and to match the output of your alternator to the quantity of amps you need to replace in that time slot. In other words, if you know you will be running the engine for two hours a day—as is normal aboard a bareboat charter boat or most coastal-cruising boats as they exit and enter anchorages—then you can plan to have that be the charging time. In addition, if you have an engine-driven refrigerator-freezer that will require an hour or more of running time every day, you can use that as the base charging time for the batteries. Ideally, if you are able to charge fully in one normal day, you will be able to discharge for two days or more without another cycle.

Most marine diesels are equipped with alternators that will spit out 50 amps at maximum output. Yet internal regulators will only charge at this rate until the batteries begin to get near a full charge. The output will then decrease rapidly until it is only 10 amps or less as the batteries climb toward their tops. Such a charging pattern will work satisfactorily on boats with only two deep-cycle batteries, divided into two banks, and a low daily discharge rate. Yet if you will be running the engine for only one hour a day to keep the fridge down or putter about harbors, then you will only be able to replace a maximum of 50 amps, and most likely you will get far less, something on the order of 25 to 30 amps. In that scenario you must then limit your discharge to 25 amps.

The simplest solution when you want to limit engine time is to use a high-capacity alternator. These come with either a built-in regulator or a separate high-capacity regulator. In the first case a 120-amp alternator will put out that full amount for the first few minutes of charging and will then have its output scaled back to a lower amount as the batteries are filled. Such an alternator will in effect generate between 40 and 60 amps in an hour when your batteries are discharged to 75 percent. This is the system we use aboard *Clover*, and it suits us well, as we need to run the engine for about an hour and a half a day to keep the freezer well down, and that time will offer us the 50 amps we normally use.

But while we are moderately happy with our system, there are much better ways to go about charging. With a high-capacity alternator working a large battery bank, it is possible to generate 100 amps or more for the battery bank per hour. The charge coming from the alternator is fed through a cycling device—of which several models are available—that starts the voltage at 15 volts or more and gradually reduces it as the batteries fill. Such a high voltage can cause batteries to heat up and gas, so it is vital that the regulator or cycle controller monitor battery temperature as well as charge rate and voltage. Also, gelcells are sensitive to high-voltage charges and need to be quick-charged at lesser values; 13.8 volts is recommended by the manufacturer.

There are many veteran offshore cruisers who swear by systems such as the Quad Cycle system or those available through Balmar, Hamilton Ferris and Jack Rabbit Marine. They find that high-rate rapid charges keep their batteries well charged and help to maintain healthy batteries for a long while.

# SIMPLE ON-BOARD SYSTEMS: THREE VARIATIONS

There are many ways of looking at on-board systems for your boat, but as we discussed above, the most straightforward is to evaluate the complexity of the systems—what gear is being run—in terms of the power required to run them. In the variations that follow, the various systems are described by two values, the average daily discharge and the total battery capacity. In each, one 100 amp/hour battery is reserved solely for starting the diesel or other emergencies. Thus, in the first system, the boat is expected to draw 25 amp/hours daily and has a house-battery capacity of 100 amp/hours, with a total battery capacity of 200 amp/hours.

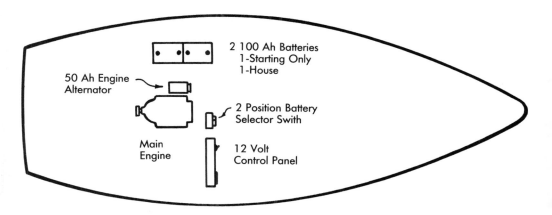

*25/200 System: In boats under 30 feet or so, it is possible to keep the systems simple and to maintain a low draw on the energy system. Yet, if planned well, even a simple system can be made to work on much larger boats.*

*25/200 System:* This system is about average for a smaller cruising boat in the 30-foot range that is powered by a lightweight 18-hp diesel with a 50-amp alternator running through a standard regulator. Given an hour a day of running time, the alternator can be expected to replace 25 amps, hence the systems on board are limited to that use. Houselights and the pressure freshwater pump would draw approximately 10 to 15 amps. Electronics such as the depth sounder, speedo/log and Loran would together draw 5 to 7 amps. And a stereo, limited use of deck lights and the VHF would account for the remaining 3 to 5 amps. While this may seem a plain-vanilla cruising boat, it is in fact sufficient in systems to sail just about anywhere. There is no reason why even much larger boats cannot be fitted out so simply and with such small and undemanding on-board systems.

When fitting out a boat of this type, it pays to look carefully at the power requirements of the instruments and fixtures you want aboard. If you can live without pressure water and will be happy with foot pumps in the galley and head, you can save money, improve reliability of the water system and cut battery drain. Similarly, fluorescent lights can cut power consumption, although they do require a large surge to start them, so switching them on and off frequently can diminish the advantages.

*50/300 System:* Although such a system could be found on boats in the 30-foot range, particularly if radar and an autopilot are to be carried aboard, such a daily discharge amount would normally be found on boats of 35 feet to 40 feet. On such a boat you would expect to find not only pressure water but also hot water taken off the engine's freshwater-cooling loop. That, of course, means there will be a shower and the need to pump wastewater overboard via a sump or bilge pump. Par pumps are most commonly used in these roles and consume approximately 15 amps while in use. So, in addition to 20 amps for houselights, you should add 5 amps (20 minutes of pump running) per day. In addition to these, sailing instruments, speedo/log, depth sounder, stereo, VHF deck lights and a Loran will add 7 to 10 amps.

The real consumer of power, however, will be an electric refrigeration unit, such as the Alder Barbour Cold Machine, which will use 20 amps or more a day. Refrigeration can be a real boon, for there's nothing like cold drinks on a hot day. Moreover, carrying ice and having to restock it every three days or so ties you to civilization. While easy to install, the efficiency of a small cooling unit depends in large part on the box it is cooling. Insulation should be at least 4 inches thick and the box itself must be small enough to remain cold for hours.

In this size range, if you intend to use radar, an autopilot or an anchor windlass, you should consider increasing your battery capacity. As it is, a high-output alternator in the 90- to 120-amp range with a

*50/300 System: When a boat begins to be of a size in which the systems require 50 amps or so daily—with 200 amp hours of backup—the need to increase the charging ability of the alternator arises. The simplest way to accomplish a higher charging rate is with a high-capacity alternator running off the main engine.*

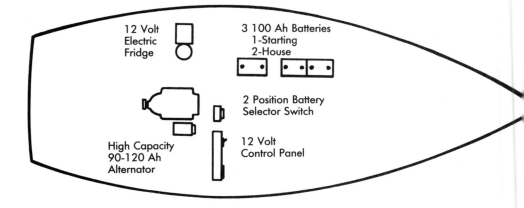

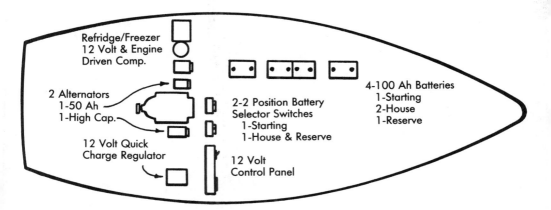

*75/400 System: In boats of 35 to 45 feet, the standard systems will draw as much as 75 amps per day. The backup battery reserve ought to be at least 300 amp hours to maintain a safety margin and to preserve the lives of the batteries. It is possible in boats of this size and complexity to begin to add systems that will make living aboard close to the comfort of home.*

standard regulator should be able to handle the load in an hour of motoring and the battery bank will have sufficient reserve.

*75/400 System:* In boats of 40 to 45 feet, which are used for coastal and offshore cruising, there is room aboard to begin to add quite an array of equipment and electronics that might have been impossible on smaller boats. It is not surprising that in the cruising fleet in the Pacific the average size of boats for couples cruising was in this range, an increase from years past. Part of the reason for the increase is the desire on the part of cruisers to take more amenities with them. As the systems grow in number and complexity, so do the needs of the engineering plant and energy systems. On such a boat, replacing 75 amps daily into a house bank of 300 amp/hours can be best accomplished with a high-output alternator of 120 to 150 amps that is driven by a power takeoff from the engine. This is in addition to the 50-amp alternator standard on the engine. With a potential output of up to 200 amps per hour, even a normal charging rate through standard regulators will provide the required charge. However, the inclusion of a high-capacity regulator with a charging monitor—such as the Quad Cycle—will improve charging and benefit the battery bank.

The standard systems on the boat—lights, electronics, accessories such as stereo and fans—will devour up to 40 amps. The refrigeration unit will have to be quite large and can in this size contain both a freezer and a cooler. To make refrigeration most efficient, it is wise to invest in a dual system that can be engine driven while the main engine is operating and then will switch to electric power for the rest of the day. On a well-insulated freezer that has a spillover to the refrigerator, you will find that an hour of engine time will only have to be supplemented by sporadic cooling from the 12-volt side. Sea Frost builds an excellent system that I was able to install myself and has served us well for two years with very little fuss. Other systems on the market that have excellent reputations are the Grunert and Crosby, which can be adapted to any big-boat application and have long histories behind them. Actual drain on the batteries will be less than with a simpler 12-volt system. An estimate for daily use of 20 amps will not be too far from the mark. It is important to keep a freezer full but not too tightly packed to get the best results. We make ice in Ziploc freezer bags to fill voids as we eat our way down through the provisions, thereby keeping us well stocked with cubes for drinks and making the freezer's job easier.

It is common on boats of this size to fit an inverter to run 110 volts through a separate wiring system. The house current can be used to operate kitchen appliances—a blender for those piña coladas—or to drive a TV and video player and a computer. Lastly, 110 volts is handy aboard for recharging the batteries in a video camera, recharging a cordless drill or operating small power tools. It makes sense to use a fairly high-wattage inverter. Units rated under 750 watts will not have enough punch to start many power tools or to drive them through hard work. A thousand watts should be considered a working minimum for general usage, and two thousand provides a margin for most on-board applications. How much power will an inverter draw? That depends entirely on use. Systems such as those manufactured by Heart Interface deliver more than 95 percent of the rated wattage, so line loss is insignificant. But an electric drill rated at 500 watts will draw 60 amps per hour of constant use. In general it will be prudent to allow an average of 10 to 15 amps per day for use through the inverter.

When setting out the battery system for a boat of this size, it makes sense to isolate batteries into three groups, one battery for starting the diesel, two for basic house use and the fourth for reserve and house backup. Two vacuum isolator switches will be necessary. When charging, high-capacity alternators work best charging a large bank, so it makes sense to link the large alternator to the three house batteries and the smaller alternator to the starting battery.

# ON-BOARD SYSTEMS FOR LARGER BOATS

Once the size of a cruising boat gets above 45 feet, the available space and the style of sailing changes somewhat. Whether cruising the coasts or offshore, boats in this range tend to require more systems and more complexity than their smaller cousins. No doubt one of the reasons for this is that most owners of boats in this range have owned and cruised smaller boats, have learned over time what works aboard and what doesn't, and have determined what gear is both desirable and necessary for comfortable and safe cruising.

Every boat in this range will be different, some dramatically so, in the way systems are organized, the methods of generating power and the priority given to gadgets and exotic devices. However, there are some general patterns that are consistent, and we'll discuss these as they apply to putting systems on board and to generating the power required to run them.

*100/600 System:* A boat of 45 to 50 feet should be considered a self-contained environment, whether at the dock or in a far anchorage. That means there should be ways of using shore power and generating sufficient power while at anchor. It means making fresh water and using a full array of navigational instruments. Most boats will have autopilots and windlasses and will be equipped to run stereos, TVs and video players. As we have shown above, when used for living aboard, it is not difficult on a cruising boat to consume 50 or 60 amps of power when running systems at a moderate rate. On a boat of this size, use in just about every category will increase somewhat, for there will be more cabin lights, more water pumps, more navigational instruments. The basic load while cruising will in general be an average of about 60 amps per day.

The big increases in loads will come from radar, the windlass, an autopilot, a larger deep freeze, a water maker and a wider array of 110-volt home-entertainment systems. Radar today is a very different animal than it was ten years ago. For cruising applications it is possible to use a small and economical unit with a range of 16 miles. This gives you a view of everything to the horizon and bit more. In active mode a radar will consume between 8 and 12 amps, which can become quite significant. Yet in standby mode modern units will draw far less and can be switched on for a quick scan and then switched off again

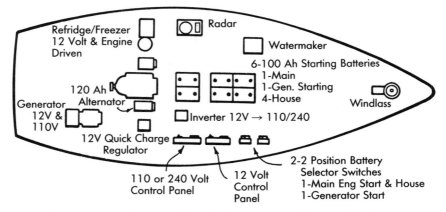

*100/600 System: On boats of 45 to 50 feet, the overall draw of the battery bank will increase over that for smaller vessels. To maintain the systems, a generator may be a wise investment. Moreover, in boats that will be used for extended cruising, supplementary systems such as solar or wind power become more attractive.*

to conserve energy. One of the more useful applications of radar aboard a cruising boat is the guard zone, which can be set to alert those on watch of a ship approaching. While leaving the radar actively on to scan a zone will entail a high power use, the function can be reserved for times when the watch is belowdecks or busy with sails. In the last BOC Round The World Race all boats were required to carry radar with the guard-zone function, and most returned from the voyage pleased with the technology—because of both shipping and icebergs. Of the smaller units Furuno, Raytheon, Apelco and Vigil are all well tested and can be bought and installed for less than $3,000.

Electric or hydraulic windlasses for handling the anchor and tackle have been developed to such an extent that it is reasonable to fit one on just about any cruising boat. Electric models, which are most common, are normally driven by high-capacity electric motors of the type used as starter motors. Power consumption can be great—up to 100 amps while exerting full force. Yet, making an allowance in the on-board systems for such a draw can mean the difference between enjoyable gunkholing and backbreaking work. Moreover, if you are sailing far and wide, an all-chain rode will be necessary, and nothing handles chain like a powerful windlass. In normal cruising the windlass will have to do its work once or twice a day. Hauling in 120 feet of chain takes about five minutes, so even if you are draining 100 amps from the battery bank, you will effectively only consume 15 to 20 amps. That's still quite a lot. Most cruising boats find that running the engine, with the alternator putting out up to 150 amps, will more than compensate for the drain. But it is good to remember that a high-capacity alternator is only putting out its maximum charge at 1600 rpm or more. The engine cannot be left in idle if you are hoping to have it keep pace with the windlass.

Autopilots consume less power when the sailing or motoring is calm, and more as steering becomes more difficult. Steaming along on a glassy sea, even the most powerful autopilot will be using very few amps an hour. Moreover, if you are steaming, you will be generating more amps than you are using. It is when sailing in rough quartering seas that the autopilot will begin to earn its keep and will consume its maximum amps. Larger models will devour 8 to 10 amps per hour, which can deplete your working reserve in only a few hours. Offshore cruising boats tend to use wind vanes for such sailing. Yet if you opt for autopilots, it makes sense to allocate a significant reserve for those times when you need up to 50 amps per day to drive the device.

A large freezer should be driven by two systems, one a power-takeoff from the main engine and the other a 12-volt system. If you can maintain the subfreezing temperature with an hour of running time on the engine, then the 12-volt system will not have to work overtime to draw the plates down and can idle along consuming few amps simply maintaining the low temperature. Still, a large freezer can require up to 50 amps or more per day with no power assist from the engine. If you plan to rest at anchor for long periods without the daily drone of the engine or generator, you will need to carry enough battery reserve for the job.

Water makers were once expensive devices that seldom found their way onto cruising boats under 60 feet or so. Today that has all changed. Water makers are becoming increasingly common on boats over 40 feet as costs come down and units become smaller and more efficient. If you plan to be self-sufficient, then making your own water through a reverse-osmosis desalinator will go a long way to freeing you from the dock. Moreover having ample fresh water will make life aboard much more enjoyable. Showering regularly, rinsing off after a swim, hosing down diving gear and windsurfer sails will all make life afloat better. Sea Recovery and Recovery Engineering are two companies leading the way. Both make units that can treat enough water daily to meet average needs, but at a cost in energy. The simplest systems that can make 35 gallons a day will use 4 amps per hour. Larger systems will treat higher quantities and create a higher battery drain. Among the cruising fleet, those happiest with their water makers are those who have to run them the least, in other words get the highest output in the shortest time period. They plan to make water while running the engine or charging the batteries for an hour or so a day and therefore don't rely on battery reserves to handle the job. To make this system work, a desalinator that puts out 10 gallons per hour will do the job nicely. On motoring days you can fill the tanks and then only top up the water while resting at anchor.

Lastly, home entertainment aboard has become very popular. TVs, stereos and video players are finding their ways onto many a cruising boat. There are models that run on 12 volts, yet 110-volt units run through an inverter or off the generator are cheaper and of better quality. While these won't consume a lot of power, you may be surprised at the drain an evening of TV can cause—up to 10 amps per hour or 30 amps for an evening of viewing.

The question of how to manage the drains on a battery system and how to replenish the batteries on a boat of this complexity is, as we said above, a personal one that can take many forms. To begin with, a boat of this type should carry six 100-amp batteries. I prefer to have the batteries broken into three groups, one battery dedicated to starting the main engine, one dedicated to starting the generator if one is aboard, and the remaining four linked into a 400-amp house bank. With two vacuum switches all three groups can be isolated or linked together in whatever configuration you want. For example, while motoring a long distance, it is good to have the alternator charging the whole system, for it will be most efficient if it is working hardest.

A high-capacity alternator of 120 amps or more will be the best choice, and in a vessel of this size, needing to replace 100 or more amps a day, you will find that an external regulator with a quick charge function will make life more enjoyable. There are several ways to measure the charge in your batteries. Simple "percent charge" meters will give you a rough idea of where the batteries stand and the charge rate from the alternator. Better than these, however, are digital volt meters, which can be tied to each battery. These will show the voltage while charging—13.8 for gelcells and up to 15.5 for lead-acid batteries—and will then monitor the drain on batteries as energy is consumed. Beyond that there are compact amp meters that will monitor your current drain and the state of each battery. If you want to keep an eye on every last amp, then this is the way to go.

In a boat of 45 feet or larger it is often possible to fit a generator into the engine compartment. New lightweight diesel units from companies such as Northern Lights, Westerbeke, Balmar and Apollo are so small and efficient that they can be tucked away fairly easily and can provide from 2.5 kilowatts to up to 10 kilowatts. For most boats 2.5 to 4.5 kilowatts will be sufficient. The generator should be able to do three things for you: provide 110 volts through the house outlets, charge the batteries through a battery charger and charge the batteries via a 12-volt DC alternator. Unless you are running an electric stove or microwave oven, the generator should be considered a backup device that can supplement electricity to the vessel and can give the main engine a day off from the task of powering all on-board systems. Those who use generators regularly are always concerned about the noise. The generator should be mounted on rubber mounts and shut away in a sound-insulated compartment. If it rumbles and roars, you may choose not to use it.

*Big-Boat Systems:* In cruising boats of 50 feet and more, the cruising systems and the power to run them are no longer dictated by the difficulties of fitting everything into a cramped space. It is common on larger boats to carry 600 amps or more in battery capacity, and many will sail with as much as 1400 amps in the system. One of the issues when dealing with so many batteries is their weight. A 100-amp battery weighs close to 100 pounds, so a bank of 1000 amps, or ten batteries, will weight half a ton. Ideally the batteries will act as ballast and should be placed over the keel and as low as possible. On custom boats it is wise to design the battery compartment into the floors over the keel.

In the above discussion we covered the systems that will cause the significant drains on the system. On a larger vessel the average daily drain can easily climb to 150 amps or more. For example, a large freezer driven solely by an electric motor on the compressor can consume as much as 75 amps daily. If a computer, a printer and perhaps a photocopier are added, then another 50 amps can be drawn from the system with only a morning's office work.

One friend of ours cruising the Pacific aboard a 60-foot schooner carries 1400 amps of battery capacity. He is in the habit of letting the Robertson autopilot do all the steering and leaves his radar on at all times with the guard zone activated. His chart tables bristle with electronics, and he runs his weather fax at least twice a day while cruising. He is active on the SSB, keeping schedules morning and night, and has all the amenities of home in the main saloon. He runs the little ship like a house and needs all the reserve he carries. He uses heavy-duty lead-acid batteries and charges with a generator and a high-capacity alternator running off the engine. His system is elaborate, but not too complicated. He is able to monitor his charging and discharge rates via simple volt meters and knows where he stands at all times. Having cruised the world for years, he knows that his bank of batteries, which he tries to keep charged to 70 percent or more at all times, will last four years, or approximately 800 cycles. He then replaces the whole bank at a cost of approximately $2,500 (1991 prices).

Another friend of ours who built a custom, heavy-displacement 51-footer for world cruising has taken a more high-tech route with his on-board systems. Because the boat is his home and office and it is intended to be so for many years, he has taken a long-term view. The heart of the system is his bank of deep-cycle, 2-volt gelcell batteries

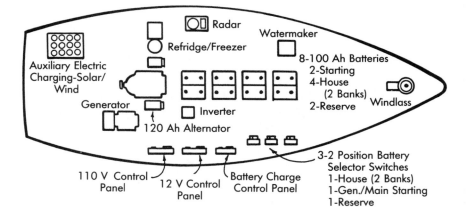

*Big-Boat Systems: In yachts of over 50 feet it is necessary to balance the almost unlimited draw of available systems with the ability and desire to replace energy to the battery banks. Running a generator and supplementing the energy reserve with alternative energy become almost a matter of course. On a boat with such complexities each skipper will have to measure for himself or herself how best to allocate resources. It is good to remember, even on boats of this size, that there is no such thing as a free amp. Every system for expending energy will require a system to replace that reserve.*

that live in two cavernous compartments on either side of the centerboard trunk. With 1200 amps in reserve, he can run all his standard equipment, make all the water he wants, run power tools and operate his office equipment, which includes a photocopier. Moreover, he has fitted the boat with electric winches, which help trim the large genoa when the wind pipes up and which can consume 50 amps or more while in use. The 2-volt batteries are the most efficient available and therefore will hold their charge for long periods, meaning he can go for days on end without having to run the generator or main engine. Moreover, with two wind-driven generators he has a steady trickle of power flowing back into the system. One of the benefits of the huge 2-volt batteries is their long life. Although he has not had to replace batteries, the gelcells should give him 2,000 or more cycles, which theoretically will be ten years or more.

On vessels of this type it becomes necessary to construct a separate battery-control panel that can be used to monitor the state of each battery and can control the flow of charge from the various charging systems. Such a control center should be wired to the nav. station if possible, where it should sit near the electrical-control panel. The batteries can be grouped into several small groups, some with dedicated purposes. Yet they should also be able to be linked into one large bank for charging. Three or more vacuum switches may be necessary to do the job.

While few cruising sailors have the desire or the wherewithal to sail with such high-tech arrangements, there is no reason not to if you are setting out to build an ultimate yacht.

## LIVING WITH THE DIESEL

As we have sketched on-board systems in the sections above, the main diesel has been the center of the power system. Most cruising boats under 45 feet are equipped with modern, lightweight diesels, while those in the larger category are often powered with traditional "tractor" diesels. In the first group, engines such as those built by Yanmar and Westerbeke have proven to be powerful, reliable and, if cared for, to have long lives. In the larger group the Perkins, Volvo and Ford diesels have proven to be solid workhorses.

There is agreement among diesel experts that a diesel engine needs to be run under load. When running without load, the cylinders coke up with unburned fuel, and gradually the residue damages rings and cylinder walls. Moreover, engines do not run well at low idle speeds, for just the same reason. Diesels are designed to work, to run at moderate revs for long periods, and to operate at relatively high temperatures. If any of these qualities are missing, then damage can be done to the injectors, the cylinders and the valves.

The problem of using the diesel as the primary source of electrical power via a high-capacity alternator while at anchor is that the alternator will only require 4 to 6 horsepower to operate at its highest capacity, and that will decrease as output decreases. In essence, once the alternator has done the lion's share of its work, the engine and alternator will virtually be freewheeling.

The addition of an engine-driven compressor for the freezer-refrigerator will add as much as 4 horsepower as well. Thus at maximum loads the engine anchor will only be using 8 horsepower of its total capacity, not enough to really heat up and efficiently burn the fuel.

The solution is to run the engine in gear if possible. Naturally when running under power, with the main propeller absorbing most of the horsepower coming from the engine and a steady running rate at high revs, the engine will be at its most efficient. If you are in a marina, one approach is to make the boat fast with heavy spring lines and to charge the batteries and run the fridge with the engine in gear. If you cannot run it in gear or are lying on a mooring or at anchor, then it is important to keep the engine's revs up to a good working level—1200 to 1800 rpm—and then to blow out the unburned fuel by upping the revs for a few minutes at the end of the cycle. Finally, if you run the engine without a heavy load on it for a long period, you will find it becomes increasingly difficult to start and will smoke badly. It is best to take the boat out and power it for an hour or more at fairly high revs—2200 or more—to clean the coking from the cylinder walls and bring the block and head up to temperature.

Running equipment off the engine will require custom installations. Most alternators and refrigerator compressors—even hydraulic units—are powered by belts running off the front of the engine. Because an engine vibrates in an oscillating pattern around the drive shaft, the pulleys on the end of that shaft driving auxiliary equipment are or should be virtually stationary. If they are not, then the engine's motor mounts are defective. From this stationary pulley, belts can be run to two or three different devices. It is common to run an alternator, compressor, a second alternator and a high-capacity mechanical bilge pump all from the engine.

Belt tension on the alternators and compressor will be critical to their efficiency, thus it is wise to attach them to the engine with double belts. If you have room in the engine compartment, a simple power-takeoff unit will enable you to drive devices mounted away from the engine. For example, if you have one alternator mounted on the starboard side of the engine, you may have room to mount the second alternator, bilge pump and compressor one on top of the other and drive these via the power-takeoff unit.

When setting up the engineering for such arrangements, all devices have to be securely attached to the hull. Should a pump or alternator break loose of its mounts, it could create havoc in the engine compartment before coming to rest. All devices will need backup belts. If possible tie spare belts to the engine—inside of working belts so that the remaining belts will not have to be removed to install a spare.

Lastly it is vital when setting up an engine compartment with extensive auxiliary equipment running off the engine to devise a way to keep the whole area clean. Should spilled engine oil, diesel, hydraulic fluid or bilge water gather in and around the engine, it can migrate into the belting systems and from them to all the auxiliary devices. The engine pump should be kept clean and separate from the bilge, and any spilled fluid should be mopped up as soon as it is spilled. There is nothing like a disposable baby diaper to soak up engine spillage. Remember to dispose of waste oil—even in a diaper—in an appropriate and legal way.

## ALTERNATIVE SOURCES OF ENERGY

The need to maintain a steady supply of power to the boat and the desire to keep engine use to a minimum has spawned a wide array of alternative choices for boosting the on-board supply of precious amps. In the offshore cruising fleet, the development of energy systems has become something of an arcane science. There are as many experts as there are practitioners, and each has a theory and an installation to suit. There are those who believe in water power, those who rely solely on solar and those who catch the wind. Some do all three.

Solar power is the least intrusive method of charging the batteries and the least efficient. Solar panels, such as those made by ARCO or Solarex, can be installed on just about any flat deck space through a diode to batteries. In most cases the panels will give only a fraction of their rated capability, even on sunny days, because the silicone wafers that convert sunlight to electricity need to be fully exposed to the sun to reach their peaks. Thus those who seek the best from their solar panels have found it necessary to install them on pivoting frames that can be swiveled as the sun wends its way across the sky.

A 40-footer with two standard ARCO panels can provide between one and two amps each per hour of sunlight, or approximately 15 to 30 amps during an eight-hour period. That's not bad for a system requiring no fuel and little maintenance. If there is room aboard for four panels, the charging output can go up to 50 amps per day or

*Solar power is the simplest way to replace energy to the system. Panels can be built onto a rack above the dodger, where they can be pivoted to face the sun. Two panels of this size will generate as much as 30 amps a day. The solar shower in the compartment forward of the dodger will heat up to 5 gallons of water for showers at no cost to the boat's energy systems.*

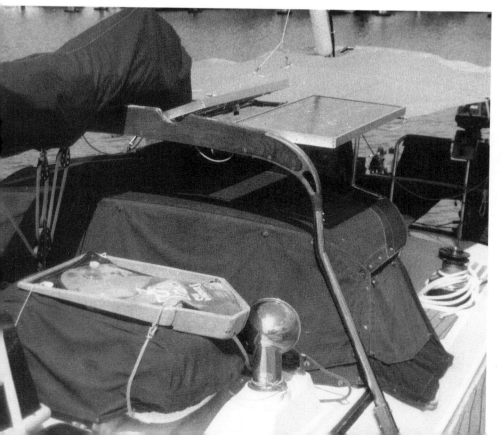

better. As a simple, passive system, solar panels are well worth the money. Yet the installation is both difficult and somewhat critical. Panels are sensitive to the angle of the sun, to shadows passing across their photovoltaic circuits and to damage from heavy objects, such as spinnaker poles and the sea.

One of the most interesting installations we have seen was aboard a 40-foot Joshua-type ketch. The boat had been cruising for ten years or so, and its owners were well versed in the intricacies of making solar power work. The panels are mounted on stainless-steel struts fixed between the mainmast and the cap shrouds. The panels can be tilted to face the sun on a horizontal axis, thus giving the best results when the sun rises and sets from bow to stern. A permanent installation that keeps the panels away from feet, spinnaker poles and boarding waves, this system seems to solve many of the problems with solar panels. For most cruising sailors, however, mounting the panels on a frame above the dodger is the best route. The panels not only get a good quantity of sun in this aft position but act as an extra spray and rain shield.

Wind power is a favorite energy source in the offshore cruising fleet. In anchorages such as George Town, Bahamas, where dozens of boats converge, we have often lain awake listening to the blades of Windbuggers, Ampairs and FourWinds slapping the air like a squadron of small helicopters on a raid. That points out both the popularity of the devices and one of the drawbacks. Windmill energy is very dependent on the strength of the wind available. When the wind is under 10 knots, most units will only provide a trickle of a few amps per hour. As the wind increases, so will the output. In a steady 18-knot tradewind, a Windbugger or FourWinds—those with long blades—will put out as much as 15 amps, which will top up batteries very quickly. In stronger winds the better windmills with long blades will begin to feather, and their output will level off. Those with smaller blades, such as the Ampair, will continue to increase output until they peak at 30 knots or so.

The installation of a wind generator can be tricky. The Windbugger, which is one of the more popular brands, is normally hoisted on a jib halyard and tied off in the fore triangle above head level. From there the charging cable can be run to a dedicated plug on the cabin top or below to a plug. If you know you will be anchored in a spot for a few days and have a fresh breeze blowing, then rigging the wind generator is worth the effort. However, with a demountable wind

*A powerful wind generator on a strut above the cockpit will function in just about any slant of wind. An efficient three-bladed prop, such as the one above, generates up to 15 amps per hour in a strong breeze.*

generator, there is the attendant problem of storing the device aboard and the hassle of getting it rigged when you do want it. Such a system is for those who want active participation in the process.

If you prefer to set up the wind generator more permanently, there are a few ways to go about it. On ketches the generator can be mounted on a bracket on the forward edge of the mizzen mast and high enough

*If you have a cockpit arch, the simplest wind generator to install will be a small unit that can operate in virtually any wind strength. While the smaller generators will produce fewer amps per hour, the ability to let them run 24 hours a day can make up for the lower charging rate.*

to be above head level. As the boat swings to the wind, the windmill will be kept into the wind and will continue to generate power. But in instances when the boat is moored bow and stern and lying across the wind, or when the boat is in a marina berth, the mizzen-mounted generator will cease to function.

Another approach that works well on sloops is to mount the wind generator on a vertical strut above the transom. The generator can be fixed to a platform that rests on bearings and can then swivel freely as the wind gusts back and forth. Such a setup requires a clumsy-looking contraption standing above the cockpit, but it does put the wind generator in the most efficient position. Moreover the device will work well when under sail, enabling you to generate power while making a passage. With such an installation, it may be wise to make the whole rig demountable, so it can be stowed away in bad weather.

The simplest installation is for smaller units such as the Ampair, which can be mounted on a strut as described above or on top of an antenna arch fitted over the cockpit. While the smaller generators do not offer the same output as those with larger blades, they will add amps to the batteries on a constant basis without your active participation and will thereby silently work away twenty-four hours a day.

How much power can you expect from a wind generator? At 15 amps per hour, a Windbugger or FourWinds will make more electricity than most boats can use, up to 300 amps or more a day. Yet as a rule you can realistically expect a larger unit to give you between 40 and 60 amps a day while in use. The smaller units will provide a maximum of 8 amps an hour in a near gale, but as a rule they will provide between 10 and 20 amps on an average daily basis.

Water power has been experimented with by many inventors and offshore sailors. While it is possible to rig a water generator that trails behind the boat and drives a generator hanging in a gimbal at the stern, the units are not widely used by offshore cruisers. Perhaps that is because of the drag induced by the propeller in the water. To get a reasonable charging rate from a water generator, the boat has to be moving at 6 knots or more, and 7 knots is a whole lot better. In a 40-foot cruising boat 6 knots is a reasonable cruising speed. Dragging a generator will cut that speed by as much as a knot, thereby increasing passage times by up to 16 percent.

Yet on larger boats with higher average speeds, water generators, such as those available from Hamilton Ferris and Jack Rabbit Marine, can yield impressive results. At a cruising speed of 7 knots the generator will induce a drag of perhaps half a knot but will return as much as 10 amps per hour. For a sacrifice of 5 miles of distance a day the generator can be dragged for ten hours and will provide the batteries with as much as 100 amps.

Water power is for those who want to reap high yields over short periods. The systems are no more complex than a wind generator and will serve passage makers in large and fast boats very well.

## Further Reading

*The Big Book of Marine Electronics,* by Frederick Graves (Camden, Me.: International Marine Publishing, 1986).

*Boatowner's Energy Planner,* by Kevin Jeffrey with Nan Jeffrey (Camden, Me.: International Marine Publishing, 1984).

*Living on 12 Volts with Ample Power,* by David Smead and Ruth Ishihara (Seattle, Wash.: Ample Power Corp., 1988).

*Offshore Cruising Encyclopedia,* by Steve and Linda Dashew (Ojai, Calif.: Beowulf Publishing Group, 1991).

# Chapter Seven

# BEATING BARNACLES AND BLISTERS BELOW THE WATER

*How to preserve the boat and get the best from bottom paints.*

▲ Basic Precautions to Prevent Blisters

▲ Renewing a Blistered Hull

▲ Beating Barnacles with Antifouling Paints

▲ Applying Bottom Paints

▲ A Total Bottom System

Twenty years ago *Sail* magazine ran a startling story about the feared "Polyestermite." It told of a new pest that had appeared on the sailing scene that was threatening to devour fiberglass boats just as toredo worms were eating older wood boats. The story mused on the fate of the sailing fleet and forecast a future of glass boats falling prey to this new modern pest.

The tale was completely apocryphal, a tongue-in-cheek bit of whimsy. In fact the humor of the piece was based on the common belief in the early 1970s that fiberglass boats were so durable, their skins so impregnable that they would never deteriorate. A charming notion. But one that we know now is a bit far from the truth.

The deterioration of fiberglass laminates because of the formation of osmotic blisters became something of an epidemic in the late seventies and eighties. In fact, during that time as many as one sailboat in four was falling prey to the real polyestermite. Companies such as Valiant, Beneteau, and Jeanneau suffered significant financial losses because their boats were too often blistering and in some cases delaminating. A war was waged by boatbuilders, and several undertook to do some basic research to solve the problem.

Everett Pearson, who runs Tillotson-Pearson in Rhode Island and is one of the most experienced fiberglass fabricators in the world, analyzed the building process from start to finish and experimented extensively with resins, cloths and building techniques. In the late 1980s he was able to offer a lifetime guarantee against blisters for all boats coming out of his factory. Moreover, working with companies such as Gougeon Brothers and the American Bureau of Shipping, Pearson pioneered the use of vinylester and epoxy resins for bottom coats. He and many of his competitors in the field now offer guarantees and are building hulls to specifications developed by the ABS.

The result is that modern cruising boats should be far less prone to blistering than those built prior to 1985. Yet the problem of living with a somewhat porous thermoplastic submerged in water for long periods is not entirely over. Even modern boats, when sanded repeatedly, scraped on the bottom or otherwise damaged by use and age, are liable to show signs of blistering and can, over time, suffer minor damage to gelcoats and laminates.

The ongoing process of protecting the bottom of cruising boats from blisters arises every time a boat is hauled for painting. So it makes sense when fitting out a vessel to attack the problem head-on and to make sure you have a complete bottom system that will not only beat the barnacles with the appropriate antifouling paints but will also protect the fiberglass hull from the ravages of long-term immersion.

## BASIC PRECAUTIONS TO PREVENT BLISTERS

The best time to apply the first level of protection on a boat's bottom is as soon as it comes out of the mold where it has been laid up. Once the mold release has been washed from the hull, a barrier coat can

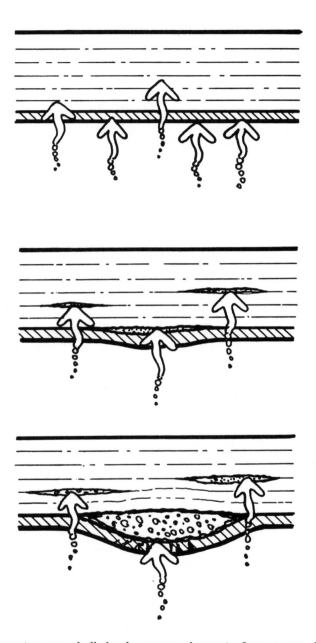

*Water migrates into some hulls by the process of osmosis. It permeates the outer gelcoat one molecule at a time and seeks voids in the laminate beneath. If dry spots or voids are found inside the laminate, then a blister can form. While most blisters are minor and occur only between the gelcoat and the first layer of laminate, it is important to repair them before more damage is done. (Illustration courtesy of Gougeon Brothers Inc.)*

be applied by the builder that will keep moisture from migrating through the gelcoat and begin the process of osmotic blistering. Some manufacturers offer this treatment as a standard part of their product, whereas others treat a vinylester or epoxy barrier coat as an owner's option. Such a barrier coat should be a high-impact epoxy such as West System epoxy or a high quality vinylester resin, which will stand a lot of wear and tear and will stand up to moderate sanding in the years to come.

Yet buyers of new boats do not have the potential problems faced by those who are buying a used boat. While a boat that has been in the water for ten or more years may never develop blisters, there is no way to predict which will and which will not.

On older boats the best system to ensure that the gelcoat and first layers of laminate remain intact is to lay up a bottom system that seals the gelcoat and is durable enough to last many years. It is important to remember that for years gelcoats have been formulated from polyester resins—orthophalic primarily—that are slightly porous. In other words, a gelcoat will very gradually permit water molecules to migrate into the polyester structure, by osmosis, and those water molecules will in time begin to react chemically with the resin. The result is a small pocket of liquid that expands and forms the blister. If left to continue, the blister can gradually migrate into the laminate and cause minor structural problems.

It is extremely rare to find a boat of ten years or more that will suddenly begin to have serious structural damage. On the whole, if a boat is going to blister badly, it will do so in the first few years in the water. Later, as the hull remains immersed, tiny blisters may form behind the gelcoat, but these are normally cosmetic and can be fixed with spot grinding and patching.

To protect an older hull from small blisters, it is necessary to grind the bottom down to the gelcoat, to remove all growth and give the gelcoat a good sanding. Because a hull will hold moisture, it is important to let the hull stand out of the water in a dry place for a month or so before treating it. If possible, the boat should sit out on a warm surface, pavement or gravel, to permit it to cook somewhat in the warmth of the sun and to retain heat through the night.

Once the bottom has been sanded, faired if necessary with an epoxy putty and cleaned, the barrier coat should be applied. Avoid applying a barrier coat when the air is too cool or in the early morning when dew and ambient moisture can still be on the hull. It is best to allow

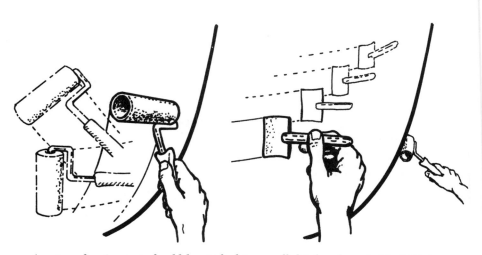

*An epoxy barrier coat should be applied to a well-dried and sanded hull. It is a tricky job best done by two people. While the first person rolls on the epoxy with a fine nap roller, the second follows with a brush to flatten any bubbles that might have formed in the wet coating. If those bubbles are not brushed out, small voids will form that can allow water to migrate toward the gelcoat. (Illustration courtesy of Gougeon Brothers Inc.)*

the hull to warm in the sun and to be thoroughly dry before starting. According to the excellent manual prepared by Gougeon, five coats should be applied to give adequate protection to the hull. Epoxy cures quickly when spread in a thin film, so it is possible to build up fresh coats on top of previous ones. Yet to get the best adhesion, the new coat should be laid on soon after the earlier coat has begun to cure. If the earlier coat is allowed to harden fully, then the bottom will have to be sanded lightly to permit the next coat to adhere.

Applying an epoxy barrier coat is a tricky job, best done by two people working together. While one rolls the coat on with a fine nap roller, a second should come along behind and lay the epoxy out with a foam brush. This will flatten the coat and, more importantly, will remove any bubbles left on the surface by the roller. Bubbles, even small ones, leave a void in the coat that can in time become a pathway for water molecules.

Once the five coats have been applied, the epoxy should be left to cure for at least a day. The bottom will have to be sanded again—with 150- or 180-grit paper—before the antifouling paint can be applied. Such a barrier coat will last many years. Yet each time you haul the boat for cleaning or painting, it is important to check the whole bottom for scratches, nicks from groundings and other abrasions. If the bottom paint has been scraped away in any places, check to ensure that the epoxy coat is still intact beneath it. If not, then a touchup will be necessary.

## RENEWING A BLISTERED HULL

Blisters are not a serious problem on most boats. Even a hull that has dozens of small blisters can be treated successfully and kept from deteriorating with occasional patching. Only when the hull becomes seriously pocked with masses of blisters and there are signs of delamination should you consider removing the gelcoat and first layer of laminate.

To repair small blisters, you have to grind the blisters down until you hit dry fiberglass. As the blisters are attacked with the grinder, the soft gelcoat will pop and fluid will bleed out. Using a soft feathering disk and 40-grit paper, you can make quick work of them. The area around the blister should be faired and all the soft laminate removed. The hull, once ground down, should then be left to dry for as long as possible to allow any moisture in the gelcoat to evaporate.

Once dry, the voids can be filled with vinylester or epoxy putty. To get the best adhesion, the Gougeons recommend wetting each void with pure epoxy before applying the putty. When the surface is fair and all the indents have been filled, each should be given a five-layer barrier coat. When it is time to apply antifouling paint, each repair will have to be sanded so that the paint will adhere.

On boats that have many blisters it may become necessary to remove the gelcoat entirely and renew the whole bottom. This is a huge task and should only be undertaken if you know you have delamination. One way to test the bottom is with a moisture meter, which will give a reading of the moisture content in the laminate. Yet such meters are not exact. If the boat still has bottom paint on it, or if it has been standing in cool weather over a damp surface, the meter can give an inaccurately high reading. If you suspect you may need to renew the whole bottom, first remove all bottom paint and let the hull dry out in a warm place for at least a week before testing it with a moisture meter. Then if the meter indicates a high moisture level, you will know that the problem you suspected is real. For the cost and trouble of removing the bottom paint, you may save yourself the much greater cost of removing all the gelcoat.

Until recently the only way to remove gelcoat and the first layer of laminate was to sandblast. This was dirty and inexact work. Toxins were released into the environment, and the bottom was left with an uneven surface. The development of bottom peelers, which are bas-

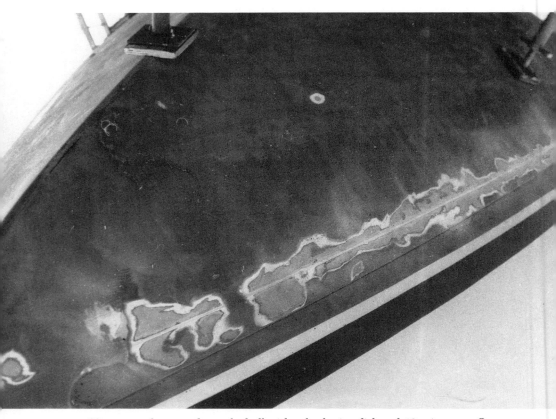

*Blisters can be ground out of a hull with a feathering disk and 40-grit paper. Once the blisters are gone, the hull should dry in a warm place until moisture in the hull has had a chance to evaporate. The voids can then be filled with epoxy putty before the final barrier coat is applied. Blisters are a cause for concern, but are rarely fatal to a well-built hull.*

ically electric planes operated either by hand or on an articulated arm, enable boatyards to cut away an exact amount of resin and glass. While still a messy job, the bottom can be peeled quickly, and the remaining surface will be smooth and even.

Once peeled, the bottom has to be left to dry for a month. Some yards will build a tent around the bottom and run dehumidifiers close to the hull. This is not particularly effective because it is almost impossible to make the tent airtight, so the dehumidifiers end up trying to dehumidify the great outdoors. It is best to leave the hull in a dry shed with a concrete floor. Over time the moisture in the hull will evaporate and the new bottom can be applied.

The easiest way to lay on a new sublevel of glass and vinylestor or epoxy is with a chopper gun. Because the layer will not normally be structural, the chopped strand and resin will provide a solid buildup without the impossible task of laying up glass mat upside down. With a new layer of glass in place and faired, the bottom can then be sealed with a barrier coat.

The cost of such a job will be significant. For a standard 40-footer you can expect to pay a professional boatyard $20,000 or more. Unless you are an expert with resins and glass, it is impractical to tackle the job on your own.

# BEATING BARNACLES WITH ANTIFOULING PAINTS

While relatively few boat owners will have to face the problem of blisters, every one of us must find the best way to keep the bottom clean. There is little debate about the effects of growth on the bottom. Aboard *Clover* a dirty bottom will slice a full knot of speed during a passage. We strive to prepare the bottom as thoroughly as possible whenever we have it out of the water, because we tend to leave the boat in tropical water for eighteen months or more at a time. That means finding the most potent paint and then putting enough of it on to last a while.

It used to be relatively easy to choose a paint to last for that period. The tributyl-tin paints available throughout the 1980s were so effective that you hardly had to repaint from year to year. Paints such as Micron 33 became famous for multiyear lives in the tropics. One friend of ours hauled his boat after three years in the Caribbean and found only a light slime, which was washed off with a garden hose.

But tin-based paints were so effective that they not only killed organisms on boat bottoms but also killed everything in the water around the boat. In 1988 the Environmental Protection Agency followed the lead of countries in Europe and around the world by banning tin-based paints for fiberglass boats. Today only aluminum and steel vessels may use the high-powered paints, while the rest of the boating community has had to find alternatives with copper as the toxic element.

The choice today is between copper-based paints with different characteristics and varying degrees of the toxin. Paints range from 20 to 75 percent copper. The quantity of copper in the paint is a direct measure of its toxic strength. Those at the higher end pack more punch than those at the lower end. And accordingly those with higher copper content will cost more.

There are two basic types of bottom paints: ablatives and conventional paints. Ablatives are soft paints that are designed to work as water moves by the hull; the painted surface slowly sluffs off the paint as it loses its toxicity. Boats that are on the move or moored in areas where there are strong currents do well with ablative-based paints.

Conventional paints leech toxin to the surface of the coating in a slow process as the paint becomes increasingly porous. These tend to be harder paints that will provide a smoother surface. But they also have a finite time over which the copper toxin will provide protection. The hard conventional paints are favored by racers and those not needing the longer service of the ablatives.

Four different bases are used to formulate copper-bottom paints; copolymer, epoxy, polymer and rosin. Rosin is the oldest base and has been in use for many years. Paints with a rosin base are hard coatings that can be scrubbed and wet-sanded for racing. Yet rosin-based paints, even those with high copper content, are not designed to last a year or more.

Copolymers and polymers have been formulated to give the longest possible service. They are soft or semisoft paints and use the ablative approach to toxicity. Awlgrip's Gold Label is a well-known polymer brand that has proved to be long lasting and effective.

Epoxy paints can be either hard or semihard coatings. Paints in this category, such as those from Pettit, are known for their long life and their ability to carry the most copper. While the heaviest of these,

Trinidad, is one of the most expensive paints on the market, it is also one of the best. Among the offshore fleet in the tropics, Pettit's products are widely used and favored by many.

Since the demise of tin paints sailors have been searching for a replacement that will do the job as well. One solution that has been found to work is adding the antibiotic tetracycline to standard copper paint. The drug is a broad-based and powerful antibiotic that doubles as a powerful biocide. Several companies market tetracycline additives for bottom paints, and these are reported to give the paint added punch.

Among the brands favored by cruisers you will find International's CSC copolymer ablative paint and Pettit's Trinidad. We have used Trinidad for two years in the Pacific and find it durable and very effective.

One of the keys to dealing with softer ablative paints is to leave them alone. It is tempting to scrub a bottom before making a passage, and this can be helpful with hard paints. But soft paints are designed to work best when the boat is moving quickly through the water, and nothing will clean the slim better than a day or two of full-speed sailing. At the end of a passage you may have picked up a few goose barnacles, but if the ablative bottom paint is still in reasonable condition, the boat's bottom will be clean. But if you attack the bottom with a scrub brush, you will accelerate the ablative process dramatically and shorten the paint's effective life span.

## APPLYING BOTTOM PAINTS

Not all bottom paints are compatible. When you have selected a paint that will be right for your area and for the type of sailing you will be doing, you need to determine if it will adhere to the surface you will be painting over. Not all paints can be applied over others of a different type.

As a rule, soft paints can be applied over hard paints that have been well sanded, but not the other way around. An ablative will begin to crumble under the veneer of hard paints, which will flake off in time. Vinyls can be used over other vinyls, but should not be used over soft paints. Rosins can be painted over all of the other types of bases, yet if you are covering a thick layer of soft paint, it must be sanded until the surface is hard. Epoxies and polymers should be applied over hard surfaces, so soft paints need to be sanded thoroughly before they are covered. However, most paints will not do well used over coatings containing graphite or Teflon. These slick racing paints are rarely used by cruising folk, but if you have purchased a used boat, you may have it on the bottom. Lastly, when in doubt, contact the manufacturer of the new paint or sand the old surface thoroughly and begin again.

On older boats it is common to find layer upon layer of paint, which in time can begin to become brittle and flake off. When the time comes to remove the buildup of old paint, the easiest way is to use a sandblaster. While this sounds complicated, most boatyards have blasters, or units can be rented from rental agencies. Using a sandblaster is not difficult. However, care must be taken to avoid blasting into the gelcoat and damaging the surface. If you have taken the trouble to sandblast the bottom, it makes sense to fair it with epoxy putty and then coat it with a barrier coat.

Most boat owners roll on bottom paint with a household roller and use a throwaway brush around the waterline and to get into the hard spots around the propeller and rudder. Using a roller is not difficult, however you must take care to apply the paint evenly and smoothly. If the paint has not been applied in a somewhat uniform thickness, it will begin to fail unevenly, and barnacles and slime will form in patches here and there along the bottom. When rolling, keep the roller loaded with paint and keep stirring the paint in the can and in the roller tray to ensure that the heavier copper is well distributed through the mixture.

More and more boatyards are spraying on bottom paint. While it is possible to achieve a very smooth finish with a spray gun, the coating can contain quite a lot of air and may be much thinner and more porous than it looks. If you are intent on spraying, it is best to use an airless spray gun. Such a gun will give the best and most even concentration of paint, while also providing a smooth surface.

Brush painting may be the best way to get a thick and even coating of bottom paint onto the hull. Those who spray or roll often find at the end of the season that the areas tipped with a brush are in the best condition. If you have the time and energy, then laying on the paint with a good 4-inch brush may be the way to go. But be careful to avoid putting on too much paint in one coating. A very thick coat will tend to become brittle and will not adhere to the old paint of the bottom as well as a moderately thick layer of paint.

How many coats should you apply? If you will be using the boat for a summer season and then hauling it again, two coats of a good-quality paint will see you through well. Should you be planning to sail to the tropics over a winter and will leave the boat in the water for a year or more, then three coats over the whole bottom and a fourth coat along the leading edge of the keel and along the waterline will give a sufficient coverage. Those traveling a long way will find that paint on the leading edges wears away much faster than elsewhere, hence you may choose to add even a fifth coat on these areas before setting out.

Among offshore cruisers it is common to lay on a different color as the base coat, so it is possible to tell quickly how far the whole surface has deteriorated. If you normally paint with blue paint, lay on a base of red. When the red shows through, you'll know it's getting time to haul out and redo the whole job.

How long will copper bottom paints really last? In the tropics and among boats that are sailed actively, we found that twelve months was about average. Aboard *Clover* we sail with Pettit's Trinidad, which has a copper content of 75 percent. We apply three coats and then add a fourth along the leading edge and at the waterline. After ten months the bottom begins to slime while sitting in harbor and then cleans itself as we are under way. At the end of a full fourteen months in tropical waters we find the coating no longer resists grasses but is still mostly effective against barnacles. This is the point at which we repaint.

Others have not had as much success. In the fleet crossing the Pacific from Panama to Fiji in 1991, many were complaining of fouled bottoms by the time they got to French Polynesia. Once the fleet had migrated west to Fiji, a fair number found it necessary to haul out for a recoating. No doubt the problem was compounded for those who sailed to American Samoa, where the harbor is badly polluted with fish tailings and sewage. Moreover, those who remained at anchor in Suva, Fiji, also polluted, found that growth on their bottoms was increasing at an alarming rate.

## A TOTAL BOTTOM SYSTEM

There are few things more satisfying than getting the best performance from a boat, whether that is quick daily runs from port to port or fast passages across the ocean. And equally satisfying is finding the bottom of the boat clean and unblistered when it is hauled out at the end of a season. The best way to achieve these ends is to make sure the bottom has a total bottom system before it goes into the water.

The best time to tackle a bottom system is as soon as the boat is purchased. If it is new, applying the full system will prevent water damage and will ensure that barnacles don't slow you down. With used boats, as soon as it comes out of the water is the time to tackle the job in order to make sure that no further deterioration takes place and to rid the bottom of all unfamiliar and possibly incompatible coatings.

As we discussed above, the first layer of a total system is the epoxy barrier coat. All blisters and gouges should be ground out and filled, and then the whole surface should be coated with five coats. We use West System epoxy because we have always found it easy to use and reliable. System Three is another choice also widely used by professionals.

Once the bottom has been coated with epoxy, it should be sanded fair and coated with two or more coatings of bottom paint. At the end of each sailing season this should be sanded virtually off to prevent a buildup and to permit you to inspect the barrier coat for damage. If you will be racing or are a demon for speed, you may want to wet-sand the final coat with 400-grit paper—hard coatings only—to get the slickest possible surface.

Treat the bottom with care and you will not only get the best performance from the boat but will ensure that the integrity of the hull is preserved.

### Further Reading

*Gelcoat Blisters: Diagnosis, Repair, and Prevention* (Bay City, Mich.: Gougeon Brothers, Inc.).

*Spurr's Boat Book,* by Dan Spurr (Camden, Me.: International Marine Publishing, 1984).

# Chapter Eight

# THE COMFORTS OF A
# FLOATING HOME

*Simple systems to make a cruising boat a better home (and invest-
ment).*

▲ The Galley

▲ The Head

▲ A Good Night's Sleep

▲ The Main Saloon

▲ Staying Warm and Dry

▲ A Boat Is an Investment

The cabin of any cruising boat is the heart of the boat. It is the place
you spend the most time and the place, if you are living aboard, you
call home. Yet in most boats it is a very small compartment in comparison to anywhere else we might choose to live. Moreover it is a
compartment that needs to be comfortable, dry and functional at
various angles and moving up and down in an ungainly way. Not even

*Although most cruising boats are serviceable for coastal and offshore cruises, only after you have added personal touches will it become a cruising home. The dinette arrangement above is excellent for families of larger crews because it permits some to sit at the table undisturbed by others moving about the boat. The use of art on the bulkheads and throw cushions adds color to the interior, and a lantern and other lights can give it a cozy ambience on a cool night.*

the pod of a spaceship drifting in orbit has to accomplish so many tasks in such a variable environment.

Yet sailors, designers and builders have over the years come up with systems belowdecks that can make this capsule a very passable home. For some sailors it is their only home. For the crew of *Clover* we once lived aboard without spending a night ashore for more than fourteen months. The environs of the cabins below *Clover*'s decks were home.

But whether you live aboard or not, there are many ways to make the interior of the boat comfortable and to give it the touch of personality that will mark it as your own place. There's a funny thing that happens once the boat has been transformed to meet an individual family's needs: Everyone starts talking about going home (to the boat) at the end of a day ashore.

In the process of giving a boat a personal stamp and making it functional and homey, there are some areas that will not only add to the crew's comfort, they will add to the value of the boat itself. The galley and the head are both areas that will benefit from sensible personal touches. But the saloon and in fact every locker can usually be made to work better and to be more comfortable, whether the boat is new or has been owned and cruised by sailors before you.

## THE GALLEY

If you have ever tried to prepare a meal in an ill-equipped galley when the boat is hard on the wind and lurching along in a seaway, you will have encountered the problems that a well-thought-out galley should overcome. The cupboards will disgorge their contents every time one is opened. Bowls and utensils will slide about and end up on the cabin sole. Water and spilled ingredients will course about the counter space and make traction underfoot tenuous. And the cook himself will be hurled about as he tries to handle hot pots and pans.

There are three conventional types of galleys: U-shaped facing athwartships; U-shaped running fore and aft; and bench-style, which runs fore and aft along one side of the hull. The athwartships galley is the most difficult to work in at sea. The cook will constantly be fighting the tendency of a boat to roll downwind, or the angle of heel when going to windward. If you will be cooking in an athwartship galley, you will need to fit a galley belt and protect yourself from falling against the stove with a grab bar.

The fore and aft U-shaped galley works better. In normal sailing conditions it is possible to wedge yourself into the space and continue to use both hands for dicing onions. A galley stove should be gimbaled on a fore-and-aft axis, so a galley of this design may expose you to the front of the stove as you work. If so, a sturdy stainless-steel bar should be in place to keep you away from hot burners and boiling liquids.

The bench-style galley works well on large boats. In boats under 40 feet such a design permits the galley to dominate the saloon so that meal preparation becomes a group endeavor instead of a one-man job. On larger boats the galley can be tucked under the side deck and cockpit. If the boat has an after cabin, then the galley can double as a passageway aft. In such an arrangement the cook is usually able to lean comfortably against one counter or a bulkhead while whipping up a meal. Like the fore-and-aft galley the stove presents a threat, so it must be behind a sturdy bar that will allow a person to hold on or fall against it when the boat leaps off a wave.

No matter which shape galley you have, it seems a law of nature that as soon as someone goes below to prepare a meal—particularly something elaborate for a pleasant dinner—the wind picks up, the seas become square and a rogue wave pattern appears from some unexpected direction. If you are cruising offshore, it is often possible to slack sheets for an hour or so to give the meal its best chance of survival. Yet no matter what you do, cooking in rough weather is a challenge.

That said, a well-fitted-out galley will help you overcome the meal-time maelstrom. First, the counters should be a hard surface that can be cleaned easily. Most builders today use Formica. While this is durable, you need to have a handy cutting surface on which to work. It makes sense, if you are upgrading the galley, to install a cutting board, fixed in place, over a fridge lid or on top of one of a pair of double sinks. The counter surfaces will be slippery, so it is important to have fiddles built across wide spaces that will catch pots and utensils when they are put down. These should not enclose spaces entirely, for you want to be able to sweep away crumbs and wipe the area down with a wet cloth.

The best arrangement for fiddles on a Formica counter is to have them removable. The fiddles should have two or more small brass rods or pegs fixed to their undersides that fit tightly into small copper or brass tubes inset into the counter. When you go to sea, you can fit the fiddles in place. And when you get into port you can remove them and store them.

Galley lockers need to be divided and then, when loaded, tightly packed. The simplest way to divide a locker is with thin battens, at least 2 inches high, glued across the locker's base. Figure out what containers the locker will normally handle, measure them and then set the battens in to hold the containers in their places. On a rough trip we once had from Fiji to New Zealand, one of the plastic containers we use to hold liquids somehow fell over behind several other containers. We didn't miss it until Rosa noticed thick treacle running out under the locker door. A half quart of the sticky ooze had spilled, which would have been humorous if it hadn't been blowing 25 knots on the nose at the time. It took all morning to clean up the mess.

Everything you use in the galley should have its own plastic container. Glass or cardboard won't hold up and will break or dissolve. The best containers we have found are made by Tupperware, Rubbermaid and Klick Klack. These can be bought in sets that nest one on top of another or stow tightly side by side. We keep weekly supplies of cereal, flour, crackers and other dry goods in large 2-quart containers with positive snap lids. Even wedged in place with dish towels, these occasionally begin to migrate about the lockers, but at least the contents stay contained and dry.

Spices, condiments and the assorted cans and containers are notoriously difficult to stow away neatly. The easiest way to deal with a dozen or more different spices is to install a full spice rack with its own tightly fitting containers at the back of a handy locker. These can be topped up from larger containers kept in a dry locker elsewhere. Small containers for items such as stock cubes, sugar, honey, treacle and so forth should be nestled together to keep them from tipping over when the boat lurches. Plastic bottles of ketchup, salad dressing and mayonnaise often have snap lid closures. Yet these will rarely stay closed if the container tips over. Once opened, these gooey fluids should be moved into Tupperware or screw-topped containers and wedged into lockers tightly.

Plates, cups, saucers and mugs all need to have their own dedicated slots. Aboard *Clover* we eat off stoneware virtually all the time, reserving plastic plates and bowls for the cockpit or beach barbecues. While china or stoneware tends to slip about a bit, we prefer the real thing because it looks better, lasts longer in normal wear and is easier to clean. To store plates, cups and saucers, we have simple racks in our lockers. These are built to fit and keep the items in place no matter what the weather. The simplest method of constructing racks for plates is to start with a 1-inch base and set four ½-inch dowels vertically from the base to hold the plates tightly. With this system if you change the plate size at some point, all you have to do is reset the dowels to accommodate the new diameters. Bowls, cups and saucers need to have built-in boxes tailored to the correct size.

Glasses and mugs often find their way onto shelves, either inside a locker or against a bulkhead. If you have room, mugs can be hung in a row on heavy brass hooks. We find that a small covering of tape on the hook will keep the mug handle from squeaking when the boat is rolling. Glasses need to be held tightly in place. The traditional method is to build a plywood holder inside a locker that has holes drilled to accept the glasses. But this uses a lot of space. We keep eight good-quality glasses in such a locker, but our everyday plastic glasses live above the galley sink on a shelf that is divided with battens.

The stove is the most important piece of gear in the galley. Years ago it was common to find kerosene or alcohol stoves on cruising boats, but today virtually everyone sails with gas, either butane or propane. There are really four fuels you can contemplate using. Alcohol is not really a viable fuel for cruising because it is impossible to replace away from home and has such a low flame temperature that it is only marginally effective. Kerosene offers the greatest cooking heat and Primus burners are both easy to maintain and repair and can be replaced worldwide. Yet kerosene is smelly, and it is often difficult to find cheap alcohol with which to ignite the burners. Butane has the next-highest flame temperature and can be used in both butane and propane stoves. Butane can be found worldwide. Propane, which is used in North America and a few other countries, has a lower flame temperature than butane, but is perfectly satisfactory in most stoves.

The trouble with butane and propane is their density. They are heavier than air and therefore will sink into the bilge if you get a gas leak. It is important, when installing either system, to store the bottles in a deck locker that drains overboard and to rig the system with a solenoid shutoff switch of the type sold by Marinetics. Gas alarms give an added measure of protection. Although commercial gases have an aromatic additive that is strong enough to alert even someone sleeping, a buzzer sounding will really get your attention.

Natural gas (CNG) is the fourth option. While this lighter-than-air fuel has gained some popularity in North America, it is not available worldwide. If you are building a boat from scratch and can design in a large compartment for the gas bottles, and you plan to stay close to supplies for the fuel, then CNG makes sense. It has the lowest flame temperature of the available fuels, so you will burn more of it, but it will not sink into the bilge and become a bomb waiting to go off.

The amount of fuel you use will depend on the type and on how you use it. Aboard *Clover* we carry two 20-pound bottles. We prefer aluminum bottles because they do not rust and have a life-span longer than steel bottles. In cold climates we use 20 pounds of propane in the galley stove every six weeks, so our supply lasts three months. In warmer climes, where we use butane instead of propane, our 40-pound supply lasts up to four months.

The stove itself should be designed for cooking both in port and at sea. Almost all modern boats will have a fully gimbaled stove with an oven. It should be in a stainless-steel-lined compartment and hung on heavy pivots that are through-bolted to the bulkheads on either side. A stove is heavy. If it were to get lose, it could kill a person or could cause a sudden gas leak. Three-burner stoves are normally the maximum size that will fit into galleys on boats under 50 feet. If space is limited, a two-burner stove can be used as well, although it is the rare cook who will enjoy such a limitation. The stove should have high steel fiddles all the way around and adjustable pot holders over each burner. One of the dangers of cooking in a seaway is falling against the hot stove or oven. If possible, it is wise to install a stainless-steel bar in front of the stove to protect the cook and to offer a grab rail in bouncy conditions.

The refrigerator should be treated just like a cabinet. If possible it should be divided with battens and shelves to permit plastic containers of various sizes to be stowed neatly. Boxes such as those made by Klick Klack are excellent for holding leftovers and will stack and stow tightly together. We use Tupperware 1-quart bottles for all liquids—except wine and beer—because they can be wedged tightly together and will not come apart, leak or break when tossed around and dropped. Inside the freezer we use Ziploc bags for everything. Meats and fish that are to be frozen are first separated into meal-size portions and then frozen. If possible we buy our meat prefrozen, which cuts down on fridge time after a large provisioning. To keep the fridge clean, we fitted a large plastic tray in the bottom, which collects all sorts of oddments over a period of three or four months between defrostings and enables us to tip the whole lot out without having to sponge out the base of the compartment. If the freezer is large enough, it is helpful to fit removable baskets that enable you to get to the bottom layer quickly and permit air to circulate between frozen items enhancing the freezing process.

The last item of galley equipment that will be found on ocean-sailing boats is a restraining belt. Such a belt is fashioned from canvas or sailcloth and should have rings and a sturdy hook in both ends for attachment to worm-eyes fixed to the bulkheads at waist level. The belt needs to be heavily attached to the furniture, for it will be supporting a person's weight and absorbing a possible fall. There are some offshore sailors who refuse to use a galley belt because it will restrain a person trying to flee from a spilled pot of boiling water. Yet after having sailed many miles with a belt and many without, both Rosa and I opt for one. It makes cooking under way much less of a chore. A safety precaution, when using a belt, is to avoid filling pots above the one-third level to ensure that they don't become top-heavy as the boat rolls or lurches.

## THE HEAD

When you think of the confined space of a cruising boat's interior, it seems a waste to sequester off one fifth of it in a compartment that is used no more than a few minutes a day. Yet a head, like a bathroom at home, is a very important space aboard the boat and deserves both ample room and care when fitting it out. Most head compartments are positioned forward and place the head itself athwartships, with a sink forward and possibly a shower device on the bulkhead opposite. Behind the head, cabinets are generally built in.

While conventional, this is not the best design for offshore sailing and cruising. When the weather is at all rough or the boat is on a heel, using the throne can be exceedingly difficult. When the U.S.

Naval Academy was designing the new 44-footers to replace the venerable Luders yawls in which the midshipmen trained for twenty-five years, one of the refinements to make it to the final design was a fore-and-aft-facing head positioned aft under the cockpit's bridge deck. The head faces forward and is positioned tightly between a bulkhead and the sink counter. When the boat is on a heel, it is still possible to sit reasonably comfortably on the throne without the threat of being tossed off. Moreover, being positioned aft, it is away from the bow sections, where the boat's motion will be the worst. It is away from most of the sleeping area so that night visits to the loo don't wake everyone else on board. And being at the base of the companionway ladder and near the engine, the compartment can also be the home of a heated wet locker. If you are designing a new vessel or drastically altering an existing boat, placing the head next to the companionway makes a lot of sense.

All heads leak. And all heads, in time, begin to have a distinct odor all their own. Both facts are only enhanced by the need on most cruising boats to have a holding tank linked into the system. The trick in living with a head is first to renew the seals on the device annually if you live aboard, or biennially if you only cruise in the summer. This won't stop the water migrating around pump handles and weeping off the bottom of the bowl, but it will slow the flood. Holding tanks need to be empty. At every opportunity it is wise to pump out the tank and then, as soon as you are in legal waters, flush the tank with salt water and a weak bleach solution.

The cabinets in a head are often the place where masses of small toiletry items collect. These have the annoying habit of falling over and emptying their contents at unexpected moments. Once, aboard our boat we were confounded by a serious-sounding hiss coming from somewhere forward of the saloon. A long hunt for gassing batteries or a ruptured holding tank finally led us to the head cabinets, where we found an aerosol can of hair mousse slowly but surely emptying itself into a plastic tray filled with razors and face creams and cotton balls. Like the cabinets in the galley, head compartments need to be broken into small sections with battens. Plastic trays that have sides at least 3 inches high can be set in place between battens, where they will stay put.

For medical supplies, plastic fishing or tool boxes work well to contain what can be a large quantity of small vials and packages of unguents, potions and bandages. The boxes should be clearly marked with their contents and fitted into shelves with battens to hold them in place.

Unfortunately the head cabinets are often also storage areas for towels and bedding. This may be the only place on the boat to keep these items, yet it is also one of the wettest areas in the interior, so fabrics will tend to mildew. To keep linens and towels fresh, stow them away in plastic bags. Small sweater bags with plastic zippers work well, as do heavy kitchen garbage bags.

By old standards a shower is a luxury aboard a boat, and most builders and designers treat it that way by either eliminating shower facilities completely or forcing sailors to shower with a phone-type nozzle while standing over the head. This might work for occasional use, but if you will be cruising extensively and living aboard for weeks at a time, then a shower will be as important to the well-being of the crew as the chart table. On boats under 40 feet or so, it is impractical to have a dedicated shower stall, although that is the best solution. If, however, you are forced to shower in the head compartment, rig a shower curtain on a track all the way around the ceiling to permit you to rinse off and wash without getting every square inch of the compartment wet. Narrow curtain track and sliders work well here. Normally you will be able to hide the shower curtain behind the head door or in a corner when not in use. By using a wraparound curtain, dampness can be kept out of the lockers and away from the head fittings and will therefore reduce mildew and cut down on dampness in the lockers.

A separate shower stall is a luxury that, once used, you soon can't live without. The compartment not only keeps all water from migrating throughout the head but also provides a space for hanging wet towels, rinsing salty clothes and even stowing gear while sailing offshore. Aboard *Clover* we have such a luxury and are thankful we do. It transforms life aboard from "camping" to relatively comfortable living. We've mastered the 2-gallon shower, which is a thorough rinse-off, a wash and a final rinse. And Rosa has become a mistress of the 3-gallon session, which includes hair and all the other things she likes to do under a stream of steaming hot water. No doubt having a shower in regular use puts a strain on the freshwater supply. While a water maker (which we don't have) would eliminate that strain, we find we can live comfortably on 50 gallons per week—for all freshwater uses.

# A GOOD NIGHT'S SLEEP

On an offshore cruising boat, nine nights out of ten are spent either at anchor or moored to a dock. Yet when you are planning to cruise far and wide, or even to make two- or three-day runs up and down a coast, the need for real sea berths becomes clear. Unfortunately most production cruising boats have not been designed for sleeping aboard while at sea. That is because there is a real difference between a good sea berth and the type of berth we want when we're in a secure anchorage. And in a boat of 30 or 40 feet it's hard to have it both ways.

A good sea berth has several distinct qualities. It should be narrow so that the occupant does not roll about. It should be near the center of the boat, where it will be subject to the least amount of motion. It should be dry and warm, which means it can't be near an open hatch, such as the companionway. And it needs to have a lee cloth to keep the sleeping sailor from tumbling onto the floor when the on-watch tacks.

The best sea berth is a pilot berth positioned outboard of the settee in the saloon. This will be near the center of the boat and should pitch less than any other berth. It will be narrow and has the hull ceiling as one side, so it is naturally snug. A lee cloth can be arranged on the inboard side that ties off securely to eyes screwed to the deck head. It is far enough from the companionway to be dry. The berth is out of the way of other crew, so it can be left made up all the time. Lastly a pilot berth can be enclosed with a curtain on a track that makes the small space into private quarters reminiscent of Pullman berths on old sleeper trains. If the boat is large enough, then having pilot berths on either side of the saloon will be a feature much praised by those who sail with you.

The next best sea berths will be the settee benches of the saloon. These are lower in the boat, so they will be less affected by rolling than pilot berths. But a settee berth is right in the middle of the cabin, prone to wetness from the main hatch and exposed to any and all activity by the on watch. This berth can be somewhat enclosed by an extra-large lee cloth, but it is definitely second best to the pilot berth.

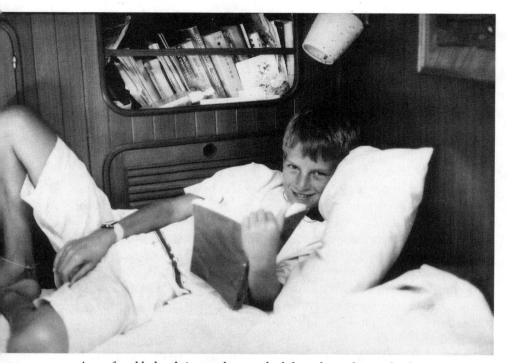

*A comfortable berth is one that can be left made up during the day and has good light for reading and space around it for storing clothes, books, and personal gear. Note the bookshelf above the berth: The books are held in place by a thin batten, which can be easily removed when you want to retrieve a book.*

A quarter berth can be a good sea berth or an unacceptable one. If the quarter berth is directly below the companionway ladder and not protected by a bulkhead, or if it is supposed to double as the navigator's seat, then it will be damp, in the on watch's path of travel and illuminated by the ship's electronics. You will have to be a very tired sailor to get any rest here. But if the quarter berth has its own space defined by bulkheads and possibly a door, it will prove to be one of the favorite berths on the boat. Although not at the center of the hull, it will have only moderate motion. With a door closed, it can be quite dry and very quiet. If the wind is howling on deck and the water rushing furiously by the hull, a quiet cabin will be very welcome to those going off watch.

Lastly, an after cabin can be an excellent place to sleep if it has sea berths, or a terrible place if all it has is a giant double bed. Big double beds are portside attractions. They have little use at sea. If you and your partner want to get together at sea, a reasonable single berth will do just as well as a queen-size platform. The best arrangement for an after cabin is to have one large berth at one side of the cabin, which can be the double berth in port, and a smaller single berth, which can be the after sea berth. If you can close off the after cabin, you will find it a dry and pleasant sanctuary that will enable you to forget the wind and weather for a while—a very nice thing to do if you have a long way to go.

We have not mentioned the forward cabin because it is a rare cruising boat that has a forecabin that can be used while at sea. The standard V-berths in most designs are pushed so far forward into the bow that they are at the point of maximum movement. Every pitch, every roll, affects the bow. Moreover the noise of the rigging, the sound of the bow wave, and the thumping of lines and feet on deck all conspire to make a person sick while keeping him awake.

Forward cabins that work at sea are positioned just forward of the saloon, with a head shoved into the forepeak. On some designs of 50 feet or more you will find two cabins side-by-side in this arrangement, with upper and lower berths in each. This is an excellent use of space and provides four comfortable sea berths.

Yet sleeping at sea is something cruising sailors do in the small offshore diversions between cruising grounds. For most of us a good berth will be one used while the boat is level, the sea and wind quiet, and the anchor well hooked in the bottom. To fill that bill, a berth needs to be comfortably soft, big enough, properly ventilated, adequately made with comfortable bedding and equipped with appropriate lights. Moreover, if possible, there should be adequate berths on board for those being slept in regularly to be left made up all the time. It should feel like home, particularly if it is going to be home for a while.

Four-inch open-cell foam is the standard mattress on most boats. While that is sufficient, a thicker mattress will offer more comfort. With modern foams it is possible to construct a sleeping mattress to suit your likes by selecting different types and laminating them together. Because the foam will be sitting on a plywood base, berths are all basically firm. If you like a soft bed but don't want your hip to bottom out on the plywood, a mattress made of a 4-inch layer of low-density foam glued on top of a 2-inch layer of high-density foam will fill the bill. If you like a flat, hard bed, the 4 inches of high-density foam will be right, unless you are very heavy, in which case 6 inches will be better. Combinations of foam can create just about any effect you like, except that saggy feel of a really old spring bed.

Foam loses its springiness with use. A mattress that feels firm under you will in time begin to conform to a body's shape. Having tried several different combinations, we have settled on a 6-inch mattress made of 2 inches of low-density foam laminated on top of 4 inches of standard foam. On top of this we put a quilted bed pad, giving the whole mattress a soft but firm feel.

If you intend to spend a lot of time on board, then you may well want to give up sleeping bags and other camping items. Sheets and pillows with pillowcases covered with either a light quilt or blankets make a berth feel like a comfortable bed. Making form-fitted sheets is not difficult. Just about every major sailing port has someone who makes form-fitted sheets and bedcovers for boats. And if you have a standard production boat, you may well be able to simply order bedding from one of the firms that advertises nationally. Percale, which is a blend of synthetic and cotton fibers, works well in the marine environment and is easy to wash and dry. It makes sense to have two complete sets of sheets on board, with the spares stowed in sweater bags or wrapped up in plastic garbage bags.

Blankets are necessary if you cruise out of the tropics. The best blankets on the market today for cruising boats are made of polypropylene. The material is similar to Patagonia's Synchilla, or the synthetic pile found lining windbreakers. In blanket form it is warm, light, easy to wash and dry and will not mildew unless left wet for a long period.

If you are having cushions made for sleeping berths, it is important to remember that the berth will be covered with bedding. Sheets alone will add about ½ inch to the size of the cushion and blankets, and bedcovers can add another full inch. Make sure new cushions are cut small enough to permit the bedding to be tucked around the edge easily. If the cushions fit neatly and tightly onto the berths when they arrive, they are too big.

The last details around a comfortable berth are lights and ventilation. Every berth on the boat needs to have a small reading light in place above it. Double berths need two lights. These can be small spotlights that take 10-watt bulbs, but they must offer enough illumination for reading when all other lights are out.

Ventilation in sleeping compartments can be supplied by open ports, a hatch cocked ajar or via a Dorade vent. A wind scoop of some type can be a boon in the tropics. Yet if you will be cruising in warm climes, small electric fans will more than earn their keep. There are several types of fans available. In our experience those that require the fewest amps are the most useful.

*Ventilation below, particularly into the sleeping compartments, galley and head, can be accomplished with Dorade vents. Note that the vent is in the after section of the box. The Dorade vents the galley below, and air is expected to flow forward through the cabin and exit via a forward hatch. Spray or rain that enters the vent will drain on deck through the limber hole at the box's base.*

## THE MAIN SALOON

These days just about every sailor in North America calls the main cabin of a sailboat the "salon." But as everyone really knows that's the wrong word. A salon is a French hall where parties are thrown and art and witticisms are displayed; or it's a place to have one's hair coiffed. An English saloon, a word that comes from the French *salon*, is also a great hall. But in maritime usage it is the large public cabin on a ship. And in American usage it is a place to drink whiskey and have fistfights, so called because inventive types in the last century decorated their drinking establishments to look like the saloons of famous ships.

So, we call ours a saloon. We have parties there and have been known to drink a nip of whiskey there and have even had a few scuffles.

A good main saloon will have to do many things well, for it is the focus of the boat's interior and the place where all the other spaces come together. It's also the place where the crew will spend the majority of its time. It should be well lighted, comfortable for eating, entertaining, reading, playing games and writing letters and journals. And it should be the place that feels most like home.

There are several arrangements for saloons common in modern cruising boats. The most traditional layout is to have a drop-leaf table down the middle, with settee benches on either side and a pilot berth above one of the settees. In the days when boats were long and narrow this was the most economical use of the limited space. Yet one side of the table is always a passageway for those going forward, so only three people could sit comfortably at the table at any one time.

On more modern boats with wider beams, the drop-leaf table has given way to built-in dinettes that can seat from four to eight or more. The beauty of a dinette is the ability of several people to sit there while others are moving about the boat. If you are entertaining or if the children are engaged in schoolwork or if one person is busy writing letters, the rest of the crew can be busy in the galley or moving about the boat without disturbing the sitters.

In dinette arrangements a settee berth is usually placed on the opposite side of the cabin, with either cabinets above it or a pilot

*Fabric in the main saloon should be durable and colorfast. The settee berth shown gets the most traffic of any seat or berth in the boat, hence it should be the model for the fabric that will be used elsewhere.*

berth. While the dinette is the main sitting area, the settee bench in fact will be the most-used seat on the boat as it is the most central. It will also take the most abuse from sunlight, dampness, spills and feet. For that reason, when selecting foam and fabrics for the saloon, the whole should be modeled on the settee.

Nothing will establish a decor in the saloon more than the fabrics used. And, doubtless, few improvements will have more effect on resale. There are literally hundreds of different fabrics used by professionals in the marine trade, from fine linens to heavy-duty industrial synthetics. On most cruising boats under 60 feet or so it is impractical to use natural-fiber material. It is susceptible to mildew and rot, stains, stretches with wear and the colors tend to fade in bright sunlight. For cushions that will be covered, berths in particular, inexpensive and durable synthetic materials are usually the best choice. Sunbrella is widely used for berths. In fact, Sunbrella is a good choice for the saloon as well if you want a simple, traditional look at a modest price. The fabric comes in a wide variety of patterns—lawn chairs and awnings are often made of Sunbrella—so you can match it to just about any scheme.

If you are looking for fabrics that will give the saloon more of a "living room" appearance, synthetics such as Herculon have proven to be durable, stain resistant and attractive. Beware of weaves that are loose, for they will tend to stretch and tear. And coarse fabrics may irritate sunburned skin. In the past few years Ultrasuede has found its way onto larger boats and those fitted out for luxury. The material is comfortable to sit on, durable and is available in a wide range of unique and interesting colors.

Foam for the cushions in the saloon has to be firm and durable. When having new cushions made, make certain that the foam you choose will not lose its shape and resiliency too quickly. The best cushions will be laminates of high-density foam on the bottom and low-density foam on the top. Six inches is the best thickness, but most saloon benches are designed to accept 4-inch cushions. On seats that will not double as berths, is makes sense to add a last third layer of foam or padding to the top outside edge of the cushion to give the seat shape and make it more comfortable.

Color schemes are a personal matter, yet those who design yacht interiors will tell you that in the confines of a cruising boat bold patterns quickly become tiresome. Instead, it makes sense to use a solid-color fabric and then lift the look of the interior with colorful patterns in the curtains and with throw pillows. While it can be a nuisance having several pillows loose in the saloon, they can double as spare sleeping pillows and are useful in the cockpit when entertaining.

Bookshelves are rarely large enough on production cruising boats, and few come equipped with a way to hold the books securely in place. With a little ingenuity it is usually possible to find a nook or two to build in bookshelves. Make sure the shelves are wide enough to accept the standard size of paperbacks and that you have room somewhere for large books, such as a dictionary, atlas or desk-top encyclopedia.

To keep the books in place while under way, a thin batten can be fitted across the front of the books fixed by small brackets at either end. When you want a volume, slip the batten out. A better system

*The main saloon can be made into an inviting place that feels like home. Pictures on the bulkheads will be a big lift to an otherwise ordinary space. Pictures can be hung with eyes fixed to the back of the frame through which the frame is screwed to the bulkhead. Or, with smaller pictures, sticky-backed Velcro can be used. Throw cushions add color and can be useful as spare sleeping pillows and as backrests in the cockpit.*

is contrived from simple brass bars that can be bent into a wide U-shape, with short pivots bent into each end. The pivots fit into holes drilled into the inside ends of the bookshelf, and the U-shaped bar fits outward around the fronts of the books in the shelf. When you want a book, lift the brass bar, which pivots in the holes, and slide the book out underneath it.

Pictures on the bulkheads will add color and personality and give the saloon a homey and personal feel. It is best to use plastic instead of glass when having pictures framed. Should you fall against the picture or if it comes loose from the wall, it will not shatter.

Fixing pictures in place can be difficult. You have to decide if you are willing to drill holes into the bulkheads. If not, you'll have a hard time hanging anything large. For smaller pictures in light wood frames it is possible to attach them securely to the bulkheads with Velcro tape that has a sticky backing. We use sticky-backed Velcro to hold cushion backs in place and have found it works well when applied around the back side of a frame to stick it to the bulkhead. But this is a temporary solution.

Hanging larger pictures requires holes and screws. With wood frames it is possible to drill a hole through the frame and into the bulkhead and then screw the frame into place. Use small squares of foam or sticky-backed pads to hold the frame tightly in place. Metal frames or frames that are too good to be drilled can be hung with small brass eyes that are attached to the backs of the frames with small screws. The frame can then be screwed to the bulkhead through the eyes.

## STAYING WARM AND DRY

Cruising in temperate climates where the temperature at night falls below a comfortable level can be a frigid experience that tests the humor of the crew. Rain and condensation can give the cabin a damp feel, and when the boat is closed up on a cold night, the simple act of breathing can add a lot of moisture to the air.

For comfort and to make the interior warm and hospitable, some form of interior heating will be appreciated by all who sail with you. Moreover, if you can keep the air dry inside the boat, you will keep the insides of lockers dry and cut down on condensation and mildew.

The simplest way to warm the boat is to use the old flowerpot technique. Place a common terra-cotta flowerpot upside down over a lighted stove burner and let it get hot to the touch. An amazing amount of air will circulate around the pot, and in a small cabin the air will soon be dry and warm. This system will even work on alcohol stoves, but the exhaust from an alcohol flame contains a lot of moisture, so the effectiveness of the pot is minimized.

A bulkhead-mounted stove—of the type made by Paul Luke or Dickinson—adds a pleasant touch to any cabin on a cold night and will provide enough warm air to keep the cabin dry and cozy. Stoves come in a variety of designs and burn with solid fuel, diesel, kerosene or even propane. Solid-fuel stoves are basically fireplaces. Luke and Dickinson make lovely models with soapstone faces and brass fittings. These are vented through the deck via a Charlie Noble, which keeps the rain out. Solid-fuel stoves are dirty beasts. The fuel—charcoal works best—is dusty and requires a bin somewhere on the boat. The ash tends to climb the stack and will create a mess on deck. When the wind is really blowing, the ash problem is aggravated to the point that live sparks may begin fluttering around the Charlie Noble. Solid-fuel stoves will not burn all night, nor can they be used safely while under way, so their use is limited to evenings in harbor. This may be enough heat for occasional coastal cruising in cold weather, but if you are living aboard or want to extend the sailing season into the spring and fall, a more constant and reliable form of heat will be needed.

Kerosene and diesel stoves come in all shapes and sizes, from simple sheet-metal potbellies to elaborate fireplaces with tile faces and stainless-steel fretwork. Most are fed from day tanks that should be mounted on deck. The tank will most likely have a pressure pump to keep the fuel flowing to the burner at an even rate. The stack will pass through the deck and should have a Charlie Noble on top to keep the weather out. Kerosene and diesel heaters need to be mounted as low as possible in the boat and as near the center of the saloon as can be arranged. The stack needs to be positioned well away from a wood bulkhead and covered with a grill to prevent burns. In some installations the heat in the stack will be insufficient to carry away the exhaust efficiently. In such cases a small stack fan needs to be installed to keep the flow of gasses moving upward and out of the boat.

A well-installed kerosene or diesel heater will warm a large space. Some models can be equipped with heat exchangers, which can then be used to keep water in the hot-water tank warm, or the water can be piped to small radiators in a cabin remote from the saloon. There are many sailors who have wintered in freezing climates with nothing more to heat the boat than a good-quality liquid-fuel heater.

Propane heaters—such as the Wolter system—have been developed to make use of the plumbing and exhaust system put in place for an in-line, on-demand hot-water system. Bulkhead mounted and fabricated of polished stainless steel, these heaters are efficient convection-type burners that put out a lot of heat for a small amount of fuel. If you are planning to use an in-line hot-water system, then the addition of a heater will involve only a bit more carpentry and a relatively small added expense.

The most efficient way to heat a boat of 40 feet or more is with a built-in diesel furnace that feeds hot air via ducts to every cabin on the boat. The Espar system, which is most popular with North American sailors, runs off the main fuel tanks and can be wired into the ship's 12-volt system. The actual furnace is compact and can be fitted beneath a berth or below the floorboards. Ducts have to be run to vents, and a source of fresh air needs to be provided to keep the burner going. Running off a thermostat, a diesel furnace will keep the boat at whatever temperature you choose and therefore can be made as efficient as you like. One of the real benefits of a forced-hot-air system is the ability to heat lockers—particularly the wet locker—from the inside. Nothing improves a wet, dark night watch than warm, dry foul-weather gear and dry boots. While a diesel furnace will be the most expensive way to go, the convenience and flexibility of such a system will more than pay for itself if you find yourself cruising and living aboard in cold climes.

## A BOAT IS AN INVESTMENT

If you have ever watched people at boat shows, you will have noticed that as they climb aboard a cruising boat, they go straight below. They may linger for a moment in the cockpit, turn the wheel, get the lay of the deck, but their real interest is the cabin belowdecks. That's the home away from home. Builders of production boats figured that out long ago and often tailor their boat-show boats to give them the homiest appearance possible.

There's no doubt that when you come to sell your boat, the same kind of attention to the details in the cabin will have the same effect. It should look inviting. A potential buyer has to be able to say to himself that he can see himself sitting at the chart table or lying on a berth. If the cabin does that, then when the time comes, you will be able to retrieve the financial investment you put into the boat.

Yet fitting out a boat for cruising is not an exercise in getting it ready to sell, even though that time will come. It is the process of tailoring your boat to your needs as sailors, as a crew and as a family. The interior space should reflect everything that makes you comfortable. It should be practical, attractive and well put together. It should be seaworthy, yet it can also be cozy.

If you have thought through the systems on board thoroughly, have planned for the types of sailing you will be doing with care, and have used the best possible gear, equipment and materials, then the boat you create will not only serve you well on the high seas but will retain its value. They say the two happiest days in a sailor's life are the day he buys a boat and the day he sells it. If you have fitted out well and used a systematic approach, all the days in between should be happy as well.

## Further Reading

*Dressing Ship*, by Janet Groene (New York: Hearst Marine Books, 1991).

*Offshore Cruising Encyclopedia*, by Steve and Linda Dashew (Ojai, Calif.: Beowulf Publishing Group, 1991).

*Spurr's Boat Book*, by Dan Spurr (Camden, Me.: International Marine Publishing, 1984).

*Yacht Style*, by Dan Spurr (Camden, Me.; International Marine Publishing, 1983).

# INDEX

Page numbers in *italics* refer to figures.

## A

Adrienne Automatic Direction Finder, 140
after cabins, 203
afterguys, 63–64
Aires wind vanes, 117, 118, *118,* 123
alcohol, as fuel, 196
alternators, 29, 112, 155, 159, 162, 165, 167, 170–171
regulators for, 157–158, 161, 166
American Bureau of Shipping (ABS), 179
American Samoa, pollution in, 189
amperage use, calculation of, 155, 156, 158
amp meters, 166–167
AMVER and Coast Guard rescue-at-sea system, 150
anchoring, 19, 28, 94–113
in coral, 94–95, 97, 98, 99, 101, 106, 110
in kelp, 99, 100, 102, 104
loads and, 96–99, *97*
in mud, 98, 99, 100, 102, 103, 106, 108

in ooze, 99, 103
in rocks, 98, 99, 100, 104, 106
in sand, 99, 100, 102, 103, 106
in variety of bottoms, 99, 100–101, 108
anchors:
Bruce, 76, 98, 101–102, *102*
cast-steel, 99, 101, 102
CQR, 98, 101
Danforth-type (standard lightweight), 76–77, 98, 100, 101, *104*
Deepset, 98
Delta, 102–103
fisherman's, 100, 101, 103–105
flukes on, 98, 100, 101, 103
Fortress, 100, 103
functions of, 101
Herreshoff, 77, 100, 103–105
hooking, 99, 100, 101, 104, 105
Luke, 104–105
lunch hook, 77
Northill, 105
plow-type, 76, 77, 98, 101, *104*
primary, *96,* 101
scope for, 101, 110
secondary, *96,* 101

anchors (*continued*)
  size of, 95–96
  stern, 77, *96*
  storm, 77, 101, 104
  stowing of, 76–77
  tensile strength of, 97–99
  types of, 76, 99–105
  yachtsman's, 100, 103–105
antennae, 89–91, *90*
arches, 89, 91–93, *92*
Autohelm autopilots, 28, 129, 130
Autohelm wind vanes, 115, 121, *122*
autopilots, 115, 126–131
  Alpha, 130
  Autohelm, 28, 129, 130
  Benmar, 130
  boat size and, 127
  circuit boards of, 130
  cockpit-mounted, 129
  function of, 127
  horsepower of, 127
  installation of, 129
  Navico, 130
  power for, 159, 160, 163, 165
  Robertson, 130
  rudder-angle controls in, 128, 130
  rudders and, 127
  sea-state control in, 127–128
  tiller-mounted, 129
  Wagner, 130
  yaw control in, 127
Awlgrip's Gold Label paint, 186
awnings, 84–85

**B**

backstay adjuster, 49
backstays, *35,* 36, 38, 49
baffles, 60
Bahamas:
  charts of, 144
  Loran system and, 141
  SSB nets in, 146
bareboat charters, 34, 154
barnacles, 30, 188, 189
  bottom paint for, *see* bottom paints
barrier coats, 179–180, 181, 182–183,
    *182,* 185, 188, 190
battens, 34, 38, 47, 60, 61, 83, 195
  end fittings for, 40

*see also* mainsails, battenless;
    mainsails, partially battened
batteries, 29–30, 91, 130
  amp meters for, 166–167
  capacities of, 154–157, 158
  deep-cycle, 155, 156, 168–169
  digital volt meters for, 166
  discharge rates of, 155, 158
  drains on, 28, 66, 112, 115, 155,
    166–167
  engine-driven charging of, 154, 157–
    158
  full charge of, 155
  gelcell, 155, 156, 158, 166, 168–169
  golf-cart, 155, 156
  isolation of, 162
  lead-acid, 155–156, 166
  lifetime of, 156, 169
  nickel-cadmium, 143, 156
  "percent charge" meters for, 166
  price of, 168
  two-volt, 156, 168–169
  types of, 155–156
  weight of, 167
battery chargers, 167
BBB chains, *105,* 108
beacons, 140
bedding, 200, 203, 204
Bermudian rigs, 32, 34, 38
Bernon, Bernadette, 11
Berwall, Hans, 119
blankets, 30, 204
blisters, 30, 178–185
  formation of, *180,* 181
  prevention of, 179–183
  repair of, 183–185, *184,* 190
blocks, *74*
board sailing, 83
boats:
  complexity of, 16
  depreciation of, 17
  as homes, 30–31, 191–213, *192, 209*
  interior of, *see* cabins
  as investment, 212–213
  reselling of, 17–18, 19, 21, 213
  selling price of, 18
  value of, 17–20, 21, 23
Boat/US, 98
boatyards, 24–25
BOC boats, 26, 72
BOC Challenge, 89

BOC Round the World Race, 45, 55, 70, 119, 164
bookshelves, 208–210
boom brakes, *35*, 42, 45, 48
booms, 60
   mainsail furling systems in, 61
   in standing rigs, 33, 45, 47
boom vangs, *35, 42,* 43, 48
bottom coats, 179
bottom paints, 30, 183, 185–189
   ablative, 186–187
   application of, 187–189
   conventional, 186
   copper-based, 186–187, 189
   epoxy, 186, 187–188
   hard, 186, 187–188
   polymer-based, 186, 187–188
   rosin-based, 186, 187
   soft, 186, 187–188
   tetracycline additives in, 187
   tin-based, 185–186
   types of, 186
   vinyl, 187
bottom peelers, 184–185
bottom systems, 30, 179, 181, 189–190
bow rollers, 76, *100,* 102, *102*
brand names, 17, 23, 103
Bristol fashion, 18–19, 25
Bruce anchor, 76, 98, 101–102, *102*
butane, 196


**C**

cabins:
   after, 203
   forward, 203
   as living space, 191–193, 203, 208, *209,* 213
   main, 201, 206–210, *209*
cap shrouds, 27, 36
celestial navigation, 133, 137
chafe, 40, 105, 106, 108
chain hooks, 108, *109,* 110
chain lockers, 77–78
chains, *see* rodes
chain snubbers, 108, *109,* 110
chalks, 76, 79–80
charcoal, 211
Charlie Noble, 211
charts, 139, 144

Chichester, Francis, 116
Chiles, Webb, 69
chronometers, 137
*Clover,* upgrading of, 25–31
CNG (natural gas), 197
coastal waters:
   East Coast of U.S., Loran system and, 141
   navigation systems for, 137–142
Coast Guard, U.S., 148, 149, 150
Coast Guard and AMVER rescue-at-sea system, 150
command centers, 132–153
communication systems, 28–29, 145–151
compasses, 142
computers, 148, 162, 167
Com-Tex Development Corp., 98
copolymer, 186
coral, 94–95, 97, 98, 99, 101, 106, 110
corrosion, 36–37, 56
CQR anchors, 98, 101
cruising chutes (single-luff, poleless spinnakers), 61, 63, 64–65
cruising sailboats, *see* boats
*Cruising World,* 9, 10, 11, 86, 98
   charts from, *97, 105*
cushions, 204, 207, 208
custom work, 24, 25


**D**

Danforth company, 103
Danforth-type anchors, 76–77, 98, 100, 101, 103, *104*
davits, 83, 88–89, *88*
Day, George, 9–10
Day, Rosa "Rosie," 9, 26, 28, 110
dead reckoning (DR), 136, 137, 143
deck boxes, 27, *79*
deck layouts, 68–93
   anchors and rodes in, 76–78
   lines and halyards in, 70–75, *72, 73, 74, 75*
   storage of gear in, 78–93, *79, 81, 82, 84, 87, 88, 90, 92*
deck organizers, 71
Deepset anchors, 98
delamination, 179, 183
Delta anchors, 102–103

depth sounders, 138, 142, 160
desalinators, 165–166
diesel engines, 169–171
diesel furnaces, 212
diesel stoves, 211–212
dinettes, *192*, 206–207
dinghies, 85–89, *87, 88*
*Dione*, 85, 86
distress signals, 149–150
Doppler effect, 142
Dorade vents, 205, *205*
downhauls, 33, 53
*Duracell*, 56


E


Edson Corp., 129
electronics, 19, 28–29, *90*
   alternative sources of, 171–177
   depth sounders, 138, 160
   in navigation systems, *see* navigation
      systems
   power for, 159, 161
   in radios, *see* radios
Emergency Position Indicating Radio
   Beacon (EPIRB), 149–150
engineering and energy systems, 29–30,
      152–177, *153*
   25/200, 159, *159*
   50/300, 159–161, *160*
   75/400, 161–162, *161*
   100/600, 163, *164*
   big-boat, 167–169, *168*
   types of, 158–169
environment, protection of, 155, 171,
      184, 186, 199
Environmental Protection Agency,
      U.S., 186
EPIRB (Emergency Position Indicating
      Radio Beacon), 149–150
epoxy, 30
   blisters and, 179, 181, 182–183, *182,*
      185, 190
   in bottom paints, 186, 187–188
epoxy putty, 183, 188
ergonomics, 71
Espar system, 212
European waters, navigation systems
      for, 140

F

fabrics:
   for saloons, 207–208
   for sheets, 204
fax broadcasts, 148
Federal Communications Commission,
      U.S. (FCC), 140, 150
fiberglass:
   blistering of, 178–185
   delaminating of, 179, 183
   sonic impulses and, 138
fiddles, 194–195, 197
*Finback*, 115
fisherman's anchor, 100, 101, 103–105
Fleming wind vanes, 118, 119, 123
flukes, 98, 100, 101, 103
foam:
   for cushions, 208
   for mattresses, 203–204
fog, 139
*Folkboat Jester*, 116
foreguys, 63, 70
forestays, 49
Fortress anchors, 100, 103
forward cabins, 203
Francis, Claire, 118
Franklin, Nick, 118
freezers, *see* refrigerators and freezers


G


galley belts, 198
galley lockers, 195
galleys, 19, 193–198
   safety in, 194, 197, 198
   types of, 193–194
gas, natural, as fuel, 197
gas alarms, 196–197
gear, *see* systems
gelcoats, 179, *180,* 181, 183, 184, 188
generators, 30, 112, 166, 167
   water, 176–177
   wind-driven, 169, 173–176, *174, 175*
genoas, 34, 49, 52, 57, 66, 78
"gold-platers," 17–18
Gooding, Betsy, 98
Gougeon Brothers Inc., 179, *180,* 181,
      *181,* 183
GPS (Global Positioning System), 91,
      128, *135,* 136, 143–145

grab bars, 194, 197
graphite, 188
Greene, Danny, 86
Greenwich Mean Time (GMT or UTC), 137, 144
ground tackle, *see* rodes
guys, 63–64, 70
*Gypsy Moth*, 116

**H**

halyards, 33, 57
    all-rope, 51, 52
    in deck layout, 70–75, *72, 74*
    rope-wire, 51–52
    tangled, 70
ham radios, 29, 147, 149, 150
Harken, Olaf, *65*
Harken sail-handling systems, 40, *41,*45, 47, *54,* 55, 56
Harrison, Brian and Judy, 85
Hasler, Blondie, 116
hawse pipes, 78
heads, 198–200
headsails and headsail systems, 49–59, *54, 58*
    conventional, 49–53
    furling of, 52
    reefing, 53
    roller furling-reefing, 26, 34, 53–59, 66, *67,* 71
headstays, 36, 49, 55, 56
heat exchangers, 211–212
Herculon, 208
Herreshoff anchors, 77, 100, 103–105
"High Seas Letter," 11
holding tanks, 199
hooking anchors, 99, 100, 101, 104, 105
hulls:
    blistering of, *see* blisters
    bottoms of, *see* bottom systems
    fiberglass, *see* fiberglass
Hydrovane wind vanes, 121–123

**I**

inverters, 162
*Islands,* 11

**J**

Jeantot, Philippe, 45
jibs, 52, 78
    high-cut working (Yankee), 49
    spitfire storm, 49

**K**

kerosene, 196, 211
ketches, 34, 96, 174
Knoos, Stelan, 119

**L**

laminates:
    in bottom systems, 179, *180,* 181, 183, 184
    of foam, 203–204, 208
lazy jacks, 22, 27, *35,* 47, 48, *48*
lead lines, 137–138
leaks, 199
lee cloths, 201
life rafts, 80–83, *81, 82*
lights:
    power for, 159, 160, 161, 163
    for reading, *202,* 203, 204
lines:
    in deck layout, 70–75, *72, 73, 74, 75*
    loose, *75*
    nylon, 78, 99, 105–106, 108, 112
    *see also* rodes
line stoppers, 71, 75
logs, 142, 160
Loran navigation system, 128, 139–142, 144, 160
Lucas, Alan, 125, 126
luff pads, 57
Luke anchors, 104–105
lunch hook anchors, 77

**M**

Magellan GPS, *135,* 144
mainsails, *42*
    battenless, 39, 40–43
    conventional, 38–48
    fully battened, 39–40, *41,* 43, 48

mainsails (*continued*)
  furling of, 47
  high aspect, 34
  in-boom furling systems for, 61
  in-the-mast furling systems for, 60–61
  partially battened, 39, 43
  reefing of, 45–47
  roach in, 34, 38, 39
  roller furling-reefing, 40, 59–61, 66
  running systems for, 43–49
  standard, 38–39, 71
  stowing of, 47
  trimming of, 43, *44*
mainsheets, *42*
maintenance, importance of, 18
Manihi atoll, coral hazards in, 94–95
marine gear, *see* systems
Mason 43, 10, 25, 95
masts, *72*
  fully battened sails and, 40
  mainsail furling systems in, 60–61
  prebend in, 36
  in standing rigs, 33, 36, 38
  stowing of, 83
  two-piece, 83
mattresses, 203–204
Mayday, 133, 134
"meat-hooks," 51
mildew, 200, 204, 207, 210
mizzen staysails, 34
moisture meters, 183–184
Monitor wind vanes, 118, 119, *120,*123
Morgan, Dodge, 59

N

natural gas (CNG), 197
Nautical Almanac, 137
Naval Academy, U.S., 198–199
navigation systems, 28–29
  for coastal cruising, 137–142
  for European waters, 140
  function of, 134–137
  GPS, 91, 128, *135,* 136, 143–145
  Loran, 128, 139–142, 144, 160
  for offshore cruising, 142–145
  prices of, 145
  SatNav, 91, 128, 133, 142–143
Navik wind vanes, 119
noise, 60, 203

Northill anchors, 105
Nuku Hiva, inaccurate charting of, 144

O

oil, disposal of, 171
"On Watch," 11
osmosis, *180,* 181
osmotic blistering, *see* blisters
OSTAR, 70, 89
outboard engines, 89

P

Pacific Asian Enterprises, 28
paints, *see* bottom paints
Pearson, Everett, 179
percale sheets, 204
Pettit brand bottom paints, 186–187, 189
phone patches, 149
picture mounting, *209,* 210
pilot berths, 201, 206–207
Plant, Mike, 56
plow-type anchors, 76, 77, 98, 101, *104*
polyester, 181
polymer, 186, 187–188
polypropylene, 204
preventers, *42,* 43–44, 48
Procyon, *65*
propane, 196, 211, 212
pumps, 171, 211
  power for, 159, 160, 163

Q

quadrants, 129
quarter berths, 202

R

racing boats, 18, 37, 38, 39, 43, 70, 89, 116
radar, 89–91, 139, 142
  guard-zone function in, 164
  power for, 159, 160, 163–164
radio insulators, 38

Radio Keri Keri, 132, 133
radios, 145–151
  dual function, 145, 146
  duplex frequencies on, 147
  EPIRB, 149–150
  ham, 29, 147, 149, 150
  high-frequency, 150
  ICOM, 147, 148
  Kenwood high-seas, 147
  licenses for, 146, 147, 149
  preselected channels on, 147
  shortwave, 29, 148
  simplex (single channel operation),
    147
  SSB, 132, 133, 146–149
  synthesized, 145
  VHF, 91, 133, 145–146, 150
RDF (radio direction finders), 136,
  139–140, 142
reefing:
  cockpit, 71
  jiffy, 45
  roller, 45
  single-line, 45–47, *46,* 71
  slab, 45, 70
reef points, 38
refrigerators and freezers, 29–30, 197–
  198
  amps used by, 160, 162, 163, 165,
    167
  engine-driven, 157, 161–162, 165,
    170
resins, 179, 181, 185
restraining belts, 198
rigs, 32–38
  Bermudian, 32, 34, 38
  conventional, 34–38, *35*
  fixed-wire, 33
  fore-and-aft, 32, 47
  fractional, 96
  gaff-headed, 34
  life-span of, 37
  rod, 37, 38
  rod vs. wire, 37, 38
  running, defined, 33
  running, standards for, 33–34
  split, 96
  standing, defined, 33
  standing, setting up of, 33, 35–36
  tension in, 36
rodes, 99, 105–110
  all-chain, 77, 101, *105,* 108, 112

all-line, 78, 101, 105–106, *105,* 108,
  112
  BBB chain, *105,* 108
  catenary bend in, 106
  function of, 105
  high-test chain, *105,* 108
  line-and-chain, 77–78, 101, 106
  stowing of, 77–78
rosin, 186, 187
rudders, 115
  low-aspect, 128
  outboard, 123
  spade, 128
  *see also* autopilots; wind vanes
Rule Industries, 98, 103
rust, 108
RVG wind vanes, 121

S

safety, 28, 146, 149, 211
  in galleys, 194, 197, 198
sail boards, 83
sailboats, *see* boats
sail covers, 53, 83
sail-handling systems, 32–67, *62*
  fully automated, 65–67
  Harken, 40, *41,* 45, 47, *54,* 55, 56
*Sailing World,* 9
*Sail* magazine, 178
Sailomat wind vanes, 115, 118, 119–
  120, 121
sails:
  downwind, *see* spinnakers
  hoisting of, 33
  racing, 38
  roller-furling/roller-reefing, 34
  as running rigs, 33
  stowing of, 52–53, 83
  trimming of, 33, 35
  *see also specific types of sails*
sail ties, 53, 64
saloons, 201, 206–210, *209*
sandblasting, 184, 188
satellite technology, 142, 143, 149, 150
SatNav navigation system, 91, 128,
  133, 142–143
Saye's Rig wind vanes, 123, *124*
Scanmar Marine, *117,* 119, 121
schooners, 96
scuba gear, 83–84

sea berths, 201–205, *202*, 206–207
Seafarer depth sounder, 138
servo-blades, 116–119, *117*, 121
settee benches, 201, 206
settee berths, 201, 206, *207*
sextants, 137, 143
shackles, 51–52, 55, *107*, 110
*She 36,* 69
sheets:
    for beds, 204
    in running rigs, 33
shore stations, 147–148
shortwave radios, 29, 148
showers, 200
shrouds, 27, 36, 40
sight-reduction tables, 137
silicone, 37
Simpson-Lawrence, 98
slime, 187, 188, 189
sloops, 34, *50,* 53, 96
snuffers (spinnaker socks), 63–64
solar power, 91, 171–173, *172*
Southam, John, 11
spillage, 171
spinnaker poles, 63–64, 65, 78–80
spinnakers, 34, 61–65, 66, 70
    single-luff, poleless (cruising), 61,
        63, 64–65
    triradial, 61, 63
spinnaker socks (snuffers), 63–64
spitfire storm jibs, 49
spreader-end fittings, 37
SSB (single sideband) radio, 132, 133,
    146–149
stainless steel, 37
stays, 36
    baby, 49
    inner, 49
    *see also specific types of stays*
steering:
    manual, avoidance of, 115, 126
    self-, 28, 116
    *see also* autopilots; wind vanes
stereo systems, power for, 159, 160,
    161, 163, 166
Stocking Island, inaccurate charting of,
    144
stoves:
    in galleys, 194, 196–197
    for heat, 211–212
struts, 89–91, *90*
Sunbrella, 207–208

surfboard, 83
Suva, Fiji, pollution in, 189
swagings, 36–37
*Sylvia,* 125–126
systems, boating:
    homemade, 20–22
    off-the-shelf, 22–24
    *see also specific types of systems*
systems approach, defined, 16


**T**

tangs, 38
Tapper, Joan, 11
Teflon, 188
telephone communications, 147, 149
television, power for, 163, 166
temperature regulation, 210–212
tension meters, 36
terminal fittings, 37
tetracycline, 187
topping lifts, 63, 64, 70
towels, 200
Transit System, 142
transponders, 138
traveler cars, 40, *41,* 60
trim tabs, 121, *122,* 123, 125–126
triradial spinnakers, 61, 63
turnbuckles, 36, 38


**U**

Ultrasuede, 208
ultraviolet, 59
undercoat, 30
Urbahn, Eric and Clara, 115
UTC (Greenwich Mean Time), 137,
    144


**V**

vangs, *35, 42,* 43, 48
vang tackles, 44–45
V-berths, 203
ventilation, 203, 204

VHF radios, 91, 133, 145–146, 159, 160
vinylester, 179, 181, 183, 185

# W

water makers, 165–166
weather fax receivers, 148, 150
weather forecasts, 148
webbing, 83
Weld, Phil, 59
Wells, Bob and Sylvia, 125–126
West System epoxy, 190
whisker poles, 65, 78–79
winches, 28, *67*, 71
    electric vs. hydraulic, 66
windage, 96, *97*
windlasses, 28, 109, 110–113, *111*
    electric, 111–112
    horizontal-axis, 112
    hydraulic, 112–113, 164–165
    manual, 110
    power for, 160, 163, 164–165
    vertical-axis, 111–112
WindPilot wind vanes, 121, 123
wind vanes, 28, 116–126, 130, 165
    Aires, 117, 118, *118*, 123
    Autohelm, 115, 121, *122*
    auxiliary rudder used by, 117, 119, 120–121, *122*, 125

boat size and, 123
custom, 125
Fleming, 118, 119, 123
horizontal-axis, 117–120, 121, 123, 125
Hydrovane, 121–123
main rudder used by, 117, 118, 119, 121, 123, *124*
Monitor, 118, 119, *120*, 123
Navik, 119
price range of, 123
RVG, 121
Sailomat, 115, 118, 119–120, 121
Saye's Rig, 123, *124*
servo-blade driven, 116–119, *117*, 121
vertical-axis, 121, 123, *124*
WindPilot, 121, 123
wire, 36–37, 38, *107*
    in rope-wire halyards, 51–52

# Y

yachts, *168*
yachtsman's anchors, 100, 103–105
"yacht style," 25
Yankee jibs, 49
yawls, 34, 96
Y-*Not*, 68–69